HERALDS
AND ANCESTORS

HERALDS
AND ANCESTORS

Sir Anthony Wagner
K.C.V.O., D. Litt., F.S.A.
Garter Principal King of Arms

A Colonnade Book
published by
British Museum Publications Limited

Colonnade Books
are published by British Museum Publications Ltd,
and are offered as contributions to the enjoyment,
study, and understanding of art,
archaeology and history.
The same publishers also produce
the official publications of the British Museum.

© 1978, Sir Anthony Wagner
ISBN 0 7141 8007 6 *(paper)*
ISBN 0 7141 8008 4 *(cased)*
Published by British Museum Publications Ltd.,
6 Bedford Square, London WC1B 3RA

Set in Monophoto Plantin Light

Printed in Great Britain by
Billing & Sons Ltd, Worcester, Guildford and London

HERALDS AND ANCESTORS

ERRATA

p. 8, line 26 – *for* Behemond, *read* Bohemond

p. 70, illustration 25. For the caption printed, *read:*
   Tabard of John Anstis the elder (1669–1744), Garter King of Arms. Acquired in 1937 through the author by the Victoria and Albert Museum, together with Anstis' crown, sceptre, chain and badges, and his son's tabard as Blanc Coursier Herald, from Mrs Blanche Ker, a descendant of the Anstis family.

p. 86, line 2 – *for* Hatleian, *read* Harleian

CONTENTS

I
ORIGINS

THE NAME HERALDRY is given to a system of personal and family devices which was developed in western Europe by the heralds in and after the twelfth century. There have been other such systems in other times and places.

From October 1659 to February 1661 John Gibbon, later Bluemantle Pursuivant, lived in Virginia as the guest of Colonel Richard Lee. 'In this remote province', as his kinsman the historian of the Roman Empire tells us, 'his taste, or rather passion, for heraldry found a singular gratification at a war-dance of the native Indians. As they moved in measured steps, brandishing their tomahawks, his curious eye contemplated their little shields of bark, and their naked bodies, which were painted with the colours and symbols of his favourite science'. 'The Dancers were painted', wrote John Gibbon, 'some *Party per pale Gu. and Sab.* from forehead to foot (some *Party per fesse* of the same Colours) and carried little ill-made Shields of Bark, also painted of those colours (for I saw no other) some *party per Fess*, some *per pale* (and some *barry*) at which I exceedingly wondered, and concluded, That Heraldry was ingrafted naturally into the sense of human Race. If so it deserves a greater esteem than now-a-days is put upon it' (*HE* 304-5).

Herodotus, writing in the fifth century before Christ, says that the Carians were the first to wear crests on their helmets and devices on their shields and that they taught this to the Greeks. Family shield devices seem to have been used in Athens in the sixth and fifth centuries before Christ. The Japanese system of family devices, called *mon*, presents close analogies to heraldry, though different in style, consisting of circular patterns, largely floral.

William Smith Ellis in his *Antiquities of Heraldry* (1869) collected with persistence and acumen examples of similar systems and instances from as many times and places as he could encompass: from ancient Egypt and Assyria; from China, Japan and India; from Mexico; from Greece, the

Roman Empire and Dark Age Europe. He believed that between all such phenomena there must be not merely links and similarities of origin but actual historical continuity. This view has not commended itself to later writers. It is certain, however, that the century of archaeological work since Smith Ellis wrote would now make possible a far more comprehensive and illuminating survey of his field, which might bring out links and analogies as yet unperceived.

We shall here be concerned, however, less with the features which link together all such systems than with those that distinguish our own heraldry from the rest. The heralds certainly had much to do with this. But here too there are riddles to solve, for other times and places besides twelfth to twentieth century western Europe have known functionaries who so resembled our heralds that their names, Hebrew, Greek or Latin, were translated by the word *herald* into English.

No one knows for certain what this word herald originally meant. Etymologically it should mean the controller of an army (and they were indeed from their first appearance often called heralds of *arms*), but this is far too grand for the first heralds we hear of, about 1170, as announcers or criers at tournaments (16). The Roman *praeco* was a crier. It may well be that Orderic Vitalis (writing in the early 1100s), was using *praeco* to translate *hiraut* or herald, when he wrote that in 1098, when the crusaders were besieging Antioch, Behemond ordered his *praeco*, who was called *Mala Corona* (so much like a later herald's name) to make a proclamation through the camp (*HE* 22). Perhaps, over long, dark ages the word went slowly downhill, like *constable*, once a great officer of state and army commander, now a policeman of the lowest rank. In the great Oxford Dictionary the first meaning of herald is 'an officer having the duty of making royal or state proclamations, and of bearing ceremonial messages between princes or sovereign powers'. That is indeed the point the heralds had reached by 1350 after a century or two of upward struggles from a vagrant, if rewarding life, of pursuing tournaments and their promoters round western Christendom from Denmark, Scotland or Ireland to Holland, Flanders or Brabant. The herald's profession overlapped the minstrel's.

There was mutual abuse, but evidently, also, much in common. The outside world was apt to confuse heralds with minstrels – no doubt to their annoyance. Payments of Edward I's reign, and even later, group heralds and minstrels together with trumpeters, harpers and even confectioners.

Already, however, there existed grander heralds than the rest, holding permanent appointments in royal and princely households. These were called kings of heralds, kings of heralds of arms, or kings of arms – at first perhaps with a touch of the same half ironical or folklore flavour as the May King and Queen, the Boy Bishop or the Lord of Misrule, but before long with a seriousness reflected in their standing and emoluments. By the fifteenth century the greatest heralds were accredited ambassadors (Plate VII) and by 1416 William Bruges, the first Garter King of Arms, was rich and grand enough to feast the Emperor Sigismund, when he came to England, at his own house at Kentish Town in Middlesex (Plate VIII).

But what could link criers, or even ambassadors, to designs distinctive of families – could link them, indeed, so closely that their name was given to the system and study of these? We have in fact three riddles to solve. First, where did the heralds come from, what was the tide that bore them up? Second, what at this particular date led to the sudden development of the system of designs called heraldry? And third, what connected the heralds with that system?

Where the heralds came from is obscure but what bore them up seems certain. It was the sudden vogue of the tournament as a training for war and an outlet for martial spirit. The heralds were criers at tournaments. They proclaimed them beforehand. They announced the entry of those taking part in them and so had to know them. And before long we see them keeping the score and playing a major part in the whole conduct of these events. Their performance of similar functions in actual war is well attested also from an early date but at first seems secondary and perhaps to grow as warfare itself adopted usages developed in the tournament. This brings us straight to the second question, the reasons for the rather sudden emergence of heraldry itself.

2
FEUDALISM

FEUDALISM IS A TERM invented by historians to describe a
phenomenon of the past. They are not compelled to agree on
what exactly they mean by it. The central reference, however, is to the grant by lords to vassals of land to be held as
hereditary fee or fief (*feudum, feodum*) on condition of the
performance of stated service, usually military service. The
key figure was the heavily armed and mounted knight, who
owed stated military service to his lord (Plate II). That lord
might be a baron, a tenant in chief, who, for his barony,
owed service of so many knights to his own lord the king.
The knights in their turn might enfeoff feudal subtenants –
until 1295 when the statute *Quia Emptores* forbade subin-
feudation.

Upon this framework of personal trust and service a
system was built up which by degrees reversed the drift to
disorder which engulfed and followed the Western Roman
Empire. The Frankish ruler Charles Martel (d. 741), the
grandfather of Charlemagne, who turned the tide of the
Moslem invasion of Europe by his victory at Poitiers in 732,
is credited with the first great step in establishing this system
by planting knights on confiscated church lands (see *LW*).
In doing so he was possibly much helped by the appearance
in western Europe at that moment of an invention previously,
it is thought, unknown there – the stirrup, which gave heavily
armed horsemen a firmness of seat and consequent impact
not possible before. In France between the eighth century
and the eleventh the class of professional warriors grew in
importance and the weakness of the monarchy of Charlemagne's descendants helped this class to close its ranks, deny
admission to newcomers and establish itself as a caste with
hereditary legal privilege.

The feudal system in this form was brought to England by
William the Conqueror. The strength of the monarchy
established by him and his successors – in contrast to the
French monarchy of that day – kept the English barons and

knights in much greater subordination to the crown than the French, so that they were never able to become a closed caste or to prevent outsiders entering their ranks. All the same, in England, as elsewhere in western Europe, the feudal barons and knights were for something like four hundred years the hereditary leaders of their nation.

It is true that already by 1200 the king's army was no longer truly a feudal army. For a century knights had been allowed to purchase exemption from their feudal duty of serving personally and providing military contingents. With the money thus accruing the king hired armies, and many of those he hired were still knights. Thus the change in the character of the knightly class – the chivalry – was neither sudden nor total. It did, however, pave the way to fresh developments, including that of a class of civilian country gentlemen, whose importance grew and reached its height under the Tudors.

The feudal pattern of war and government, which allotted so conspicuous a part to mounted and heavily armed hereditary warriors, each the leader of his own contingent, could well, one sees, create a demand for military ensigns and identification marks which would be those of military and territorial units and of families at one and the same time. That feudalism should produce heraldry is not surprising. The surprise is that it seems to have done so only at so late a stage in its own life. Negative evidence must be used with caution but the Bayeux tapestry decidedly suggests that no coherent system of shield, pennon or banner devices existed in 1066 and other evidence points the same way. On the other hand there is converging evidence, mainly from seals, to show that from soon after 1125 the use of consistent hereditary devices on seals and banners was spreading among the greater lords of England (Plate XIV), northern France and the Rhineland, with outliers as far afield as Tuscany, Spain and Tyrol (1-15). The enamel plate of about 1150 at Le Mans commemorating Geoffrey Plantagenet, the ancestor of our kings, is the oldest coloured example of heraldry known to me (Plate I). By 1200 heraldry was well established over a wide area and by 1250 the foundations of its grammar and system were firmly laid (Plate III).

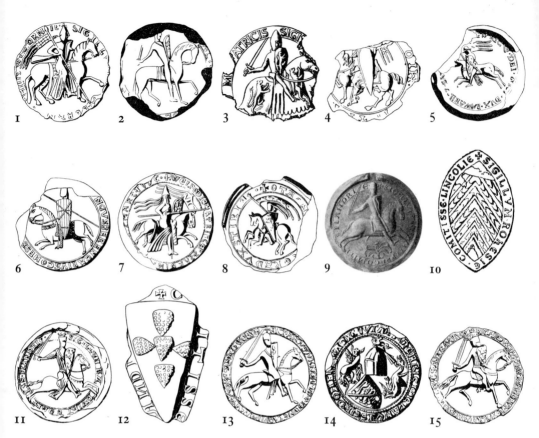

1 Seal of Waleran, Count of Meulan and lord of Worcester, 1141-2. British Library. Harleian charter 45.i.30. *ME* 339, 341-2. Banner and horse trapper checky, shield plain.

2 Seal of Gilbert de Clare, Earl of Hertford, 1141-6. P.R.O. Duchy of Lancaster Charter A. 157. *ME* 340, 342-4. Shield chevronny.

3 Seal of William FitzEmpress, brother of King Henry II of England, 1156-63. Stenton, *Early Northamptonshire Charters*, 24-6. *ME* 347, 349. Banner and horse trapper, A lion rampant.

4 Seal of Amadeus III, Count of Savoy, 1143. *Archives héraldiques suisses*, 1925, 11. *ME* 342. *DLG* 23, 38. Shield plain, banner, A cross.

5 Seal of Henry the Lion, duke of Saxony, 1144-6: son-in-law of Henry II of England. *DLG* 23, 38 (1942 ed. p. 26); *ME* 342, 347. Shield, a lion rampant.

6   Seal of Ramon Berengar, count of Provence, King of Aragon, 1150. Blancart, *Iconographie des sceaux et bulles . . . des Archives départementales des Bouches du Rhône*, 1860, pl. 2; Sagarra, *Sigillografia Catalana*, i (1922). Pl. V; *ME* 342-4; *DLG* 23, 38. Shield, Three pales. The diagonals are the strengthening of the shield.

7   Seal of Welf VI, marquis of Tuscany, 1152. *Archives héraldiques suisses*, 1916, 57. *ME* 343; *DLG* 23, Shield, A lion rampant.

8   Seal of Ottokar III, marquis of Styria, 1159. Anthony von Siegenfeld, *Das Landeswappen der Steiermark*, 1900, 142; *ME* 344; *DLG* 23, 38. Shield, A panther.

9   Seal of Philip, count of Flanders and Vermandois. 1162. Raadt, *Sceaux armoriés des Pays Bas*. Bruxelles, 1898-1901, Vol. I, 454; Demay, *Inventaire des sceaux de la Flandre*, 1873, No. 138 bis. A lion, on shield, on side of helm, and on lance banner.

10   Seal of Rohese de Clare, countess of Lincoln, 1156. *Topographer and Genealogist*, I. 318-9; *ME* 374: *DLG* 23. The earliest known heraldic seal of a woman. Entire field of vesica shaped seal, Chevronny.

11   Seal of Baldwin, count of Flanders, 1197. Demay, *Inventaire des sceaux de l'Artois et de la Picardie*, 1875-7, No. 52; *ME* 353; *DLG* 173. Lion on shield. Modelled lion statant or passant on top of helm. The earliest known rendering of a modelled crest.

12   Seal of Maud of Portugal, countess of Flanders, 1189. Demay, *Inventaire des sceaux de la Flandre*, 1873, No. 142 bis. *ME* 374; *DLG* 42, 43. On an escutcheon (earliest known for a woman), Five escucheons bezanty (Portugal).

13   First great seal of Richard I, King of England, 1189. *ME* 347, 349. Shield, A lion.

14   Seal of Henry, Earl of Lancaster, 1300. On the barons' letter to the Pope. *ME* 353, 354. Shield, England differenced with a bend. Crest on helm. A dragon. In the flanks of the seal two dragons, an early example of badge beasts as supporters.

15   Second great seal of Richard I, King of England, 1198. *ME* 347-49. Shield. Three leopards, henceforth the arms of England.

Among factors, which, it is suggested, may have been at work at this period, but not earlier, three may be mentioned: the crusades, beginning in 1095, which brought the knights of different nations together; the rapid development of the tournament in which both heralds and heraldry had conspicuous parts to play (16, 17) and the flowering and swarming of the Normans, a people at this time of outstanding energy and creativity, among whom some at least of the first steps in heraldic usage were taken.

16 Pen drawing *c.* 1560 of a joust showing two heralds in the stand and two on horseback umpiring and scoring. One of a series illustrating the Ordinances, statutes and rules for jousts made by John Tiptoft, Earl of Worcester, Constable of England, 29 May 1466, by the King's command. A section of College of Arms MS. M6 (at f. 56), a manuscript, pictorial precedent book of ceremonies, begun by Thomas Hawley, Clarenceux 1536-37, and continued for Sir Gilbert Dethick, Garter. A related collection is in the British Library (p. 9). *HCEC* 86. Pl. XIII.

17 Original cheque recording the points scored by combatants at a joust 17 November 1584, the anniversary of Queen Elizabeth I's succession. Among the combatants were Sir Henry Lee, Lord Willoughby and Sir Philip Sydney. One of a collection of original jousting cheques in the College of Arms. On the method of scoring see Sydney Anglo, 'Archives of the English Tournament: Score Cheques and Lists', *Journal of the Society of Archivists* ii (1961), *HCEC* 26, Pl. XIII.

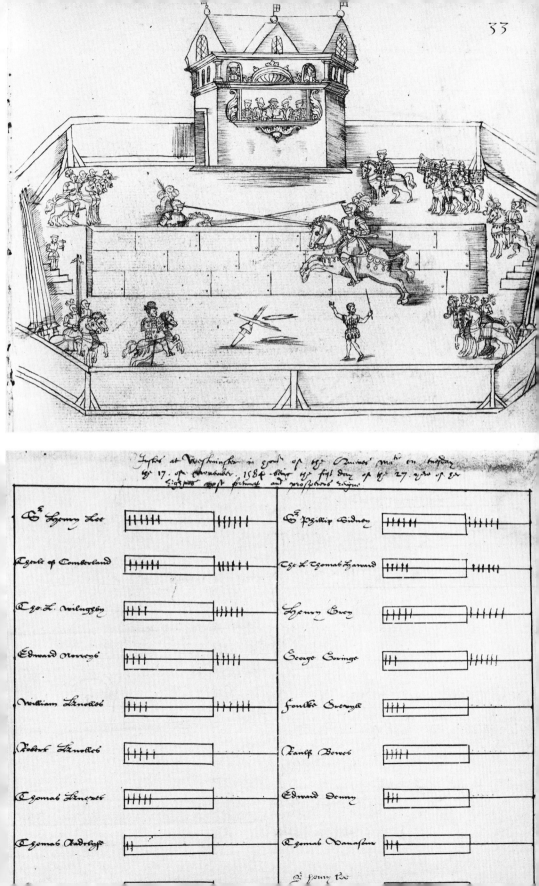

Iustes at Westminster in [honor] of the Quenes ma[jes]tie on tuesday ye 17 of [November] 1584 being ye first day of ye 27 yere of [her] [highnes] most [happie] and [prosperus] raigne

Name	Score		Name	Score	
Sr Henry Lee	IIIIIIIIII	IIIII	Sr Phillip Sidney	IIIIII	IIIII
Earle of Comberland	IIIIIIIIII	IIIIII	The L. Thomas Haward	IIIIII	IIII
The L. Willughby	IIIII	IIIIII	Henry Grey	IIIIIII	IIIIIII
Edward Norreys	IIIII	IIIII	George Goringe	IIII	IIIIII
William Knolles	IIIII	IIIIIII	Foulke Grevyll	IIIII	
Robert Knolles	IIIIII		Ranlf Bowes	IIIII	
Thomas Knevet	IIIII		Edward Denny	IIII	
Thomas Badnesse	III		Thomas Vavasor	IIII	
			Sr Henry [Le]		

NOTES ON THE COLOUR PLATES

I   Enamel plate depicting Geoffrey Plantagenet, Count of Anjou (d. 1150), son in law of King Henry I of England and father of King Henry II; probably made soon after his death; formerly in the cathedral at Le Mans, now in the Museum there. On his marriage in 1127 to the Empress Maud, Henry I's daughter, Geoffrey was knighted by his father in law who hung about his neck a shield painted with golden lions, a description which fits the shield shown on the enamel. The enamel and its history are discussed by Geoffrey H. White, *CP*. Vol. XI, App. G, and by Robert Viel, *Les origines symboliques du blason*, Paris, 1972, Ch. 2. Geoffrey's elder son, Henry II, used arms, but we do not know what. The seal of his younger son William shows a single lion on the shield. Lions rampant and passant figure variously in the arms of Geoffrey's descendants, the six lions, as in the enamel, being borne by his bastard descendants the Longespee Earls of Salisbury. *ME* 145-7.

II   Stained glass window in Chartres Cathedral depicting John, Count of Montfort l'Amaury (d. 1249), or his uncle Simon de Montfort, Earl of Leicester (d. 1265). He bears a shield, *Gules a lion queue fourchée argent*, and a banner *Party indented Gules and Argent*. Both devices were used by more than one member of the family, both in France and England. *ASP*. II 18, 115, *HHB*. 35), though the tinctures are not consistently given. The banner device was later used in England for the Honour of Hinckley, which belonged to the Earls of Leicester, and is an element in the arms granted to the City of Birmingham in 1889. The use of different devices on banner or gonfanon and shield by great lords is found in several early instances and has been variously explained.

III   Shields from a roll of arms of *c.* 1270-80, known as the Heralds' Roll, College of Arms MS. B. 29. *CEMRA* 10.

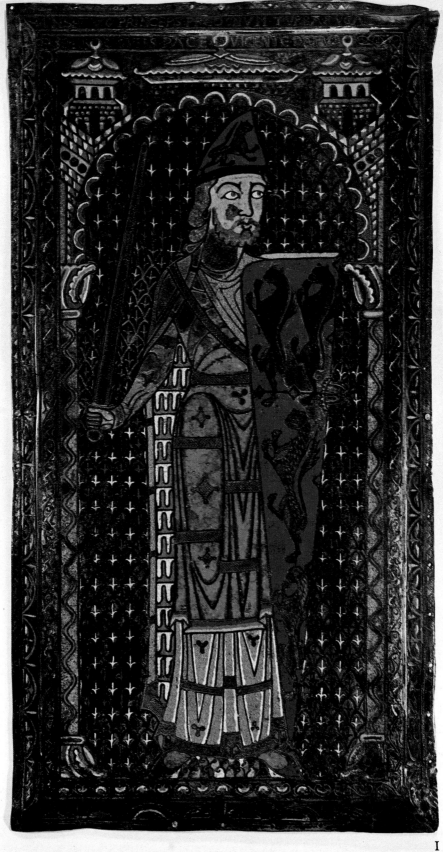

I

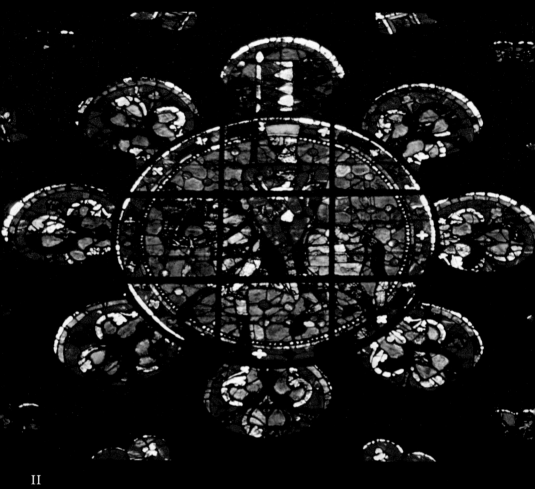

II

Henry treigoz · Robert de Ufford · Jon de benchamp · Paus Valice · Robert de munbart

Robert fix Water · Henry de percy · Nichole de le Huet · Jon le fix Jon · Patrik de Chaurci

Richard de Croft · Jon le fix geroud · Richard Hilward · Jaus de Bonby · Sire Jon vel col

Willem Bardolf · Willem marmyun · Phillip or myun · Paus de Wauci · Joffrey de escuintle

Jon de bhele · Robert Corbet · Robert de mortimer · Jon le Estrange · Willem de lesburne

III

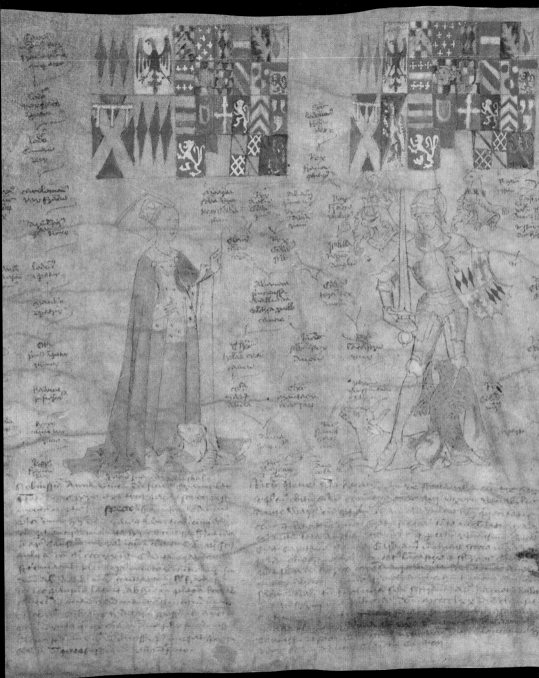

IV

IV   Banners of many quarterings, figures, pedigrees and narrative histories, from the chronicle roll of the lords and Earls of Warwick, painted and written *c.* 1477-85 by John Rous, chantry priest of Guy's Cliffe, Warwickshire; the Latin version has been since 1786 in the College of Arms. The English version, since 1955 in the British Museum (now in the Department of Manuscripts, the British Library) is a translation and fair copy probably prepared under the direction of Rous. The figures are Alice, Countess of Salisbury (d. 1462), daughter of Thomas Montagu (d. 1428) and wife of Richard Nevill (d. 1460), Earl of Salisbury; her son, Richard Nevill, Earl of Warwick and Salisbury (d. 1471), 'the Kingmaker'; his daughter, Isabel (d. 1476); and her husband, George, Duke of Clarence (d. 1478). The many quarterings in the banners represent the many lordships accumulated by successive marriages to heiresses. In the next century quarterings were given the purely genealogical significance of representation in blood. *CEMRA* 116-20; *ASP* II 277-8.

V   Shields from Cooke's Ordinary of Arms (the property of Sir Anthony Wagner), the oldest known original ordinary of arms in existence, *c.* 1340. See p. 27; *CEMRA* 58-9.

VI   Book of Tournaments of King René of Anjou, Paris, Bibliothèque nationale, MS. français 2692, f. 13, painted *c.* 1460-65. The King of Arms of the Duke of Brittany, wearing a tabard of his arms (Ermine) presents to the Duke of Bourbon (wearing and seated upon his own arms) a roll painted with the arms of eight lords proposed by his master as judges of a tournament. Two pursuivants with him wear small escucheons of their master's arms, a travelling substitute for tabards.

VII   One of a fifteenth century series of paintings depicting the legend of St Ursula. In this the Ambassador of Britain, painted as a fifteenth-century English herald, wearing a tabard of the royal arms of that date, presents a letter to King Maurus. Bruges, Couvent des Soeurs Noires, Painting No. 50612.

3
SYSTEM, RECORD AND PROTECTION

ANY SYSTEM of distinctive marks which provides for more than quite small numbers must meet certain requirements if it is to work. The marks must be so designed as to provide for an extensive range of simple yet distinctive permutations; they must be centrally recorded so that the distinctiveness of new designs can be ascertained; and there must be some provision for their legal protection. All this will be easier if some or all of these things are looked after by a professional group. How, when and by what stages the heralds came to undertake these duties we need not here discuss in detail. But there is an obvious logic in their progression from incidental connection through expert knowledge to official responsibility (fully discussed in *HH* and *HE*).

The first clear evidence of the reduction of heraldry to system is the appearance round about 1250 of the earliest of the written and painted records we call Rolls of Arms (*CEMRA* and *ASP* II). These are of several types. In those we call Illustrative Rolls the heraldry is not the primary object but is added by way of marginal adornment to chronicles, cartularies, liturgical books and even account rolls. Such are the shields with which Matthew Paris (d. 1259), the monk and chronicler of St Albans, illustrated his manuscript books between about 1244 and 1259. Most of the heraldry is painted in the margins beside notices of the persons in question in the text. There is also, however, a whole page with representations of thirty three named shields on the face and forty two on the back.

From the late middle ages we have another splendid illustrative roll, composed, written and painted in two versions between 1477 and 1491 by John Rous, a chantry priest of Guy's Cliffe, Warwickshire (Plate IV). This is not a book but a true roll (or rather two rolls) of vellum, more than twenty feet long. It is a chronicle of the lords of Warwick Castle from ancient British times down to Rous's day. The first of the two rolls in date is, I believe, the Latin version, now in the College of Arms. It has on the face sixty-six coloured drawings of figures of Kings of Britain, royal and other benefactors to Warwick and Earls of Warwick, with histories of their lives written below and shields and banners of their arms painted above. The English version, now in the British Library, is a slightly simplified, more highly finished and less spontaneous rendering of the same.

Quite different from such illustrative collections are the rolls which seem to be heralds' working tools and records. Some of these are simply records of those present on particular occasions, usually battles, sieges or tournaments (Plate VI). The oldest known records the knights at the battle of Falkirk in 1298 and their arms. The best known and most unusual is the poem which describes in French rhymed couplets the knights present in July 1300 at Edward I's siege of Caerlaverock Castle and their arms, which in some copies were painted in the margins. Dr Denholm-Young called it 'perhaps the last attempt by anyone in England to be a herald as well as a minstrel'.

The oldest and largest class of these heralds' records are what are called General Rolls (Plate III), collections comprising the arms of sovereigns of the world, earls, lords and knights. Some have a plan; others look as if the compiler, after a planned beginning, had added more or less haphazard what came his way. Nevertheless they have for the most part the look of working collections, and the same applies to the small class of Local Rolls, dealing with some one locality. For instance, the Dering Roll of about 1275 consists mainly of Kent and Sussex arms.

The last class, that of the Ordinaries of Arms (Plate V), is preeminently one of working records, for in an Ordinary the shields are grouped by the subject matter of their design: coats with lions together; coats with crosses together; coats with chevrons together, and so on. This seems to be an English invention, for outside England no mediaeval example has yet been found, whereas we have four great examples dating from before 1420, comprising respectively 644 shields (Cooke's, *c.* 1340), 556 (Cotgrave's, *c.* 1340), 1611 (William Jenyns', *c.* 1380) and 1595 shields (Thomas Jenyns', *c.* 1410).

Before – even well before – the first appearance of Rolls of

Arms, which was about 1250, the evidence of seals shows heraldic design developing its characteristic features: the bold, linear figures; the stylized birds, beasts and monsters; the sharp colour contrasts secured by the general use of six tinctures only; the fondness for simple puns on names; above all the exquisite, simple balance of the designs, adapted essentially to the triangular shield form. In fine the Normans set upon their heraldry the same masterly imprint as on their architecture.

Other elements came in later, some more admirable than others; fourteenth century pomp and splendour, fifteenth century flamboyance, early sixteenth century floridity. Then, with antiquarianism and scholarship, came a reversion to simplicity which in England saw the Stuarts out. A notable feature of early heraldry was the adaptability of its shield devices to display on banners, pennons and standards (Plate XV). Hence, incidentally, the heraldic nature of most national and many other flags. The best known design ever to issue from the College of Arms may well be the Union Jack or Flag.

After Stuart times changing taste and successive styles had some impact on heraldry. Late eighteenth century landscape, mid-Victorian clutter, late Victorian 'button makers' heraldry' had each its day. But the end was a strong reversion to older models, a recognition that in heraldry, upon the whole, those who came first did best.

Two connected non-aesthetic elements had and have also an important part in promoting this bias towards simplicity and archaism – property and heredity. Heraldry is a practical system of distinctive recognition marks. To be clearly distinct and clearly recognizable at sight is those marks' primary function. To rob them of simplicity and boldness can soon defeat that function. For the first designs to be simple was easy because they were first in the field. The more there were the harder it became to make the new ones distinctive. But with effort and ingenuity it could and can be done, and successive ages have come to see that this effort must be made.

Over and above this, but pushing the same way, is the power of the hereditary aspect. Where certain families have special prestige, their family marks will have it too, and so, to a lesser extent, will other marks of a similar kind. Hence 'the boast of heraldry' and all the connected snobbish manifestations. Snobbery begins where falsehood enters. Respect for rank, ancient lineage and the like may be criticized as foolish, worldly, servile and much else, if one happens to be of that mind. But snobbery is something different again and begins only when accidental trappings are mistaken for essence and valued accordingly. Where exactly falsehood in such matters starts can produce endless and sometimes interesting discussions. Whether noble families, for instance, have better genes or better manners than others, is a fair subject for argument. But to value a fictitious pedigree or a coat of arms to which one has no right is surely more snobbish than sensible. Such behaviour, however, is thoroughly human and its historical effects cannot be ignored.

Arms might be usurped innocently. About 1253 Glover's Roll records that William le Fort of Vivonne in Poitou and Chewton in Somerset and Matthew de Columbers of Hampshire and Wiltshire were bearing the same arms, *Argent a chief gules*. At the siege of Caerlaverock in 1300 Brian Fitzalan and Hugh Poyntz bore identical banners, *Barry or and gules*, which led to a dispute between them.

From the fourteenth century the Court of Chivalry (i.e. Court of the Knighthood, the body of knights) took cognisance among other matters of *Pleas of Arms*, that is actions at law concerning armorial bearings, and in this court the Constable and the Marshal of the realm were judges. Since the office of Constable lapsed in 1521 the Marshal (now the Earl Marshal) has been sole judge. The Constable and Marshal, and so later the Earl Marshal alone, had authority over the heralds from the fifteenth century, if not earlier. A time came when the Crown decided that the protection and control of armorial bearings should no longer be left to private action alone. Our knowledge of how arms were in early times devised and assigned is all too slight, but there is evidence that in the fourteenth century, if not earlier, lords conferred them on their adherents. Occasionally the king did so and towards the end of the century Kings of Arms were assigning or granting arms, doubtless by authority, though the oldest surviving document of grant by a King of Arms dates only from 1439. From that time on such patents of arms grow frequent and a right from the Crown to issue them was explicitly asserted from 1467.

In France by the eleventh century the knights had, as we saw, crystallized into a hereditary caste with legal privilege, to which entry thereafter could in theory only be by royal authority. In England the strength of the post-conquest monarchy, and other factors perhaps also, prevented such crystallization and kept the class structure fluid, so that the confusion of classes has been called the most striking feature of English Society in the early middle ages. There has always therefore been much movement of families both up and down the social scale.

The use of armorial bearings, however, had an original association with knighthood. Later, when tenants by knight service purchased exemption from knighthood, this extended to families of knightly standing though their members might not be actual knights. Members of this class of the highest rank below the knights were called esquires, while the rest came to be known in the fifteenth century as gentlemen.

The nearest English equivalent of the continental nobility was thus the gentry, who were in principle considered eligible for armorial bearings. The first explicit measure of control we know of was an order made by Henry V in 1416 that, whereas in recent foreign expeditions many whose ancestors never bore them had taken to themselves arms and tunics of arms called *cotearmures*, none was now to do so, save by ancestral right, or by grant from some person having sufficient authority thereunto, excepting also those who had borne arms with the king at Agincourt. This last refers to the story, told by a French chronicler and referred to by Shakespeare (who may have had it from Elizabethan heralds when he secured a grant of arms to his father in 1596), that the king promised before the battle to ennoble all those of his company there who were not already noble, and in token gave them leave to wear the Collar of SS (*HE* 36).

Kings of Arms in the fifteenth century took an oath on

creation which required them among other things to know and register the arms of the noble gentlemen in their provinces. In 1498-9 Henry VII gave Garter and Clarenceux Kings of Arms a licence 'to visit the arms and cognisances of gentry and to reform the same if it were necessary and according to their oath and bond made at their creations'. This process of heraldic visitation was put on a more formal and effective basis by the issue of letters patent in 1530 and thereafter at frequent intervals down to 1686.

4
VISITATIONS

THEIR CONCERN with inherited family marks must from an early date have given the heralds some interest in family history and it has been suggested that as peerage claims had begun to offer a field for genealogists before the death of Edward II, the heralds' help in these may have been enlisted in the later fourteenth century. The first positive evidence I have found of genealogical research by them is of the middle fifteenth century (Plate IX). From about 1480 we have pedigree books of their compilation including prototypes of the later Visitations.

It was, however, the Visitation work of the sixteenth and seventeenth centuries that made English heralds, from that time on, professional genealogists such as their predecessors and most of their counterparts elsewhere never were. In the earlier stages much of the work was romantic and amateurish – some indeed fraudulent. But as time went on the standard of skill and scholarship rose steadily to the heights attained by Dugdale in the seventeenth century and Cokayne in the nineteenth.

The development of Visitation machinery and procedure deserves closer study than it has yet had and should one day form the subject of a major treatise combining social and administrative history with that of genealogical studies. In 1530-32 Thomas Benolt, Clarenceux, in the south, Thomas Tonge, Norroy, in the north, and William Fellow, Lancaster Herald, as deputy to the former in South Wales and Herefordshire and to the latter in Lancashire and Cheshire, visited the gentry in their homes, where they looked to be entertained, travelling in summer, on horseback, with attendant servants.

The king's letters patent or writ of aid issued to Benolt called on 'all manner noble estates as well spiritual as temporal' and 'all mayors, sheriffs, bailiffs, constables and all other our officers, ministers and subjects' to render him all help in his intention 'to visit among other your arms and cognisances and to reform the same if it be necessary and requisite and to reform all false armory and arms devised without authority'. Tonge seems to have had no writ of aid though he needed it more if we may judge from experiences of his deputy Lancaster Herald in Lancashire. 'Sir John Townley of Townley Knight' Fellow wrote, '. . . would have no note taken of him, saying that there was no more gentlemen in Lancashire but my lord of Derby and Monteagle. I sought him all day riding in the wild country and his reward was ij s. which the guide had the most part and I had as evil a journey as ever I had'. 'Sir Richard Houghton Knight . . . hath put away his lady and wife and keepeth a concubine in his house, by whom he hath divers children, and by the lady he hath Ley Hall; which arms he beareth quartered with his in the first quarter, he says that Mr Garter licensed him so to do, and he gave Mr Garter an angel noble, but he gave me nothing nor made me no good cheer, but gave me proud words'.

Benolt prepared his Visitation books in advance, drawing blank shields at the head of each page; in these he tricked the arms of heads of families, alone and combined with those of their wives. Below he entered short narrative genealogies; sometimes also the fees paid. From these rough copies he had handsome painted copies in folio prepared on his return. Fellow in South Wales and Herefordshire made also some 'church notes', including tricks of arms in the windows of the friars' churches of Cardiff, Carmarthen and Brecon and drawings of figures in the church at Abbey Dore.

A Visitation begun in London in 1530 by Hawley, Carlisle Herald, and continued by Benolt himself, was not concerned with the arms of the living but with the King of Arms' right and duty to deface or 'take for his own behoof' all false armory and arms devised without authority set up in churches.

In 1561 William Hervey, Clarenceux, 'rode and took his journey into Essex and Suffolk on his Visitation and part of Norfolk and Rouge Croix rode with him and a few of his servants in his livery and badge'. Hervey's Visitations were much more extensive and more thorough than Benolt's. In 1563 he was still visiting the gentry in their homes, for a warrant of that year from a Sheriff to Bailiffs of Hundreds orders them to attend Clarenceux 'so long as he shall be within your circuit and orderly to direct him to every gentleman within the same hundred'. By 1566, however, the Sheriff was sending the Bailiffs a list of 'gentlemen and others' whom they were to warn to appear on a stated day at the house of one of their number, thus speeding the process up.

By 1583 there was further elaboration. The sheriffs or undersheriffs of counties kept lists of freeholders liable for jury service (18-20). From these they extracted for the heralds' purpose the names of those described in them as *Knight, Esquire,* or *Gentleman.* Separate lists were then made for each Hundred in the County and these the King of Arms or his deputy (a herald or pursuivant) would send to the bailiffs of the several hundreds together with warrants requiring the bailiff to summon the gentry on the list to appear before the King of Arms or herald, at a time and place named 'in the chiefest town in the hundred', bringing with them their arms, pedigrees and evidences. At the later Visitations the place was sometimes still a private house but more often an inn, and in ancient market towns it may be noted that the principal inn is often the same now as it was then. Sir William Dugdale about 1680 said that the place should be not more than six or seven miles from the home of any person summoned to it. It was Dugdale's custom to

18-20 Original papers relating to the Visitation of Gloucestershire 1682-3.

18 Printed form of Summons, completed in manuscript, by Henry Dethick, Richmond, and Gregory King, Rouge Dragon, deputies to Sir Henry St George, Clarenceux, requiring the Bailiff of the Hundred of Berkeley, Gloucestershire, to summon before them at the Crown Inn, Wotton under Edge, for Tuesday 28 August next, persons who failed to answer a previous summons, dated 27 June 1683.

19 List of those to be summoned to Wotton under Edge 28 August 1683, with notes of excuses and results.

20 Page of annotated impressions of seals produced as evidence of right to arms at the Visitation.

To the *Bayliff* of the *Hundred of Berkeley*

WHereas by virtue of his Majesties Commission under the Great Seal of *England*, directed to Sir *Henry St. George* Knight. *Clarenceux* King of Arms, you did receive a special Warrant under ~~our~~ *his* hands and Seals, ~~bearing~~ *of Chester Herald and Rougedragon Purs.vt marshalls and Deputies to the said Clarenceux, bearing* date the *fifth* day of *July* — last, authorizing you to warn divers persons residing within the said Hundred of *Berkeley* to make their appearances before ~~us~~ *him* at the *Sign of the Lamb* in *Dursley* ⌐ on *Tuesday* the *Eighth* day of *August* last, as well for the Regiſtring their Deſcents, and juſtifying their Titles of *Eſquires*, *Gentlemen*, &c. as their right to ſuch Coat^s of Arms and Creſts which they uſually ſhew forth and bear. And whereas notwithſtanding ſuch your notice, there are ſome amongſt them who have not as yet made their appearance accordingly. Theſe are therefore by virtue of the ſaid Commiſſion further to charge and command you, That you immediately repair to every ſuch perſon whoſe name is expreſt in the Schedule annex'd, and warn them to appe~~a~~r before us ~~Thomas May~~ *Henry Dethick* Eſq; ~~Chester~~ *Richmond* Herald, and *Gregory King Rougedragon* Officers of Arms, Marſhalls and Deputies to the foreſaid *Clarenceux* at the ~~~~ *K. Crown* in *Wotton* ⌐ ~~aforesaid~~, on *Tuesday* the 28th day of *August* next : Letting them know that in caſe they, or any of them, ſhall refuſe ſo to do, we muſt be enforced to Adjourn them to attend the Earl-Marſhal of *England*, or his Deputy, to anſwer their Diſobedience and Contempt of His ſaid Majeſties Commiſſion.

Given under our Hands and Seals [at] the College of Arms *London* this 27th day of *June* ⌐ in the 35th year of the Reign of Our Soveraign Lord Charles the Second by the Grace of God, King of *England*, *Scotland*, *France* and *Ireland* Defender of the Faith, &c. Annoq; Dom. 1683 ⌐

Henry Dethick Richmond.

Gre ry King Rougedragon

Berkeley Hundr.   Wotton Tousday 28. Aug. 1683

Co: Glouc:

Aylingdam — Ric. Yate gt. X lives sometimes in Glouc — Sent a lre to acquaint us he was sundowed
          to Badminton

Acington — Joseph Yeomans X — said he was no gent, but an Attorney desired to be Excused
          for he could not come.

Edmondsbury — Tho. Chester ar X Sum. in pson.
            Jn°. Sumers Vic X Sum. sent. by his man.

Bradley — Rob:
        Rich. Mandy gt — Head Bayliff of ye Ht. (no gt.)
        Rob. Oldsworth Esqr. dead since entred, one will: Clutterbuck, of Bristol bought ye Esta   sometime Sheriff
        Tho. Burton Cler X Sum. in pson by his father. (no gt.)

Cam — Raph Willet   must find Esredd, one Hicks of Somersett will have ye Estate
     after the death of Mrs Willet

Cromhall — Mr. Gregory Cler X Sumd. Sent, the prebend of Gloucester - Entred before —
         Tho. Hicks — X Sum. p Ticket. y
         Mr. Stokes — gone into — Hundred.
         John Howell X Sum.

Dorsley — als y — Will. Purnall X   John Arundell X
                                     Francis Whitney } Sum: left at their houses.   Purnall said he could
                                     Tho. Bailey. — dsd.   not come nor would

Hampfallow — Mr. Dan. Lycense dead a Citizen of Glouc E
           Jn°. Morse gent a poor man
           Jn°. Clutterbuck dead a yeoman in estate

Ham — Walter Lloyd X Sum. by his man. a Welchman My D. Berk: keeper of New park

Horfield — Edw. Hancock Cler. would not be seen a Noncon. Minr. Son of a Blacksmith

Hinton — Edw. Samiger vil Sawiger. very poor and decayed, of ancient yeomanry

Kings Wotton — Sr. Robt. Southwell Knt X A note left with his Tenant —
             Lady Hook — X left a note with her Tenant but she lives not there.
             Mr. Goring X sent a note by the minr.
             Thomas Hearh vil Hayne, lives at Weymouth com Dorset, a Capt. in ye Militia here

Nympsfield — Will. Bridgman gt X Sum. in pson a gent.
           Giles Estcourt Att X Sum. in pson a gent.

Newton Bagpath — Joseph Pointz gent X Sum. in pson Entred before, ye same as of Uley — (App.)

North Nibley — Mr. will: Archard X very sick for a great while no gent. onely married John Smith of Nibley, dau
             Mr. Will. Smith X Sum. in person son of will. 3d. broth of Old John. ye Justice.

Cambridge — Dr. Edw: Diggell DD X said he would not come. a Bachelor aged 70 or upwards —
          Has not (ridd) 7 miles in a day this 7 years

Stinchcombe — Mr. Purnall , qf not Mr. Rous's Clerk
            Mr. Hopton no such man
            Tho. White at London, a life gardener

Uley — Geo. Small X Sum.

Standford — Mr. Tho. Wise X left a note at his house

Wotton under edge — Mr. Tho. Dawes fil. X Sum. no gt.
                  Mr. Robt. Dawes patr X o (ye Elder uero at Beaumisgraud)
                  Edw. Wallinckon Sum
                  Tho. Burton gt — fath: of ye parson of Bradly - (a Schoolmar) (no gt.)

Wortheline — John Nelme gt. 40. Sum. in person - R.

(left margin notes):
Magistraty
  notice
during the
  to be
ion

Very auncills of this County

Brixton of Avning.

palie diu ... azure ... lyons ... Cumberol and ... Maryland gules —

Mr Sheppard of Hamptons Seal.

Stephens & Legg

with of Wibley in countie of Gloue:
Pedegree begining with Wm Smith.
Humberston & ending with John was pro
ed to us ye 2 day of Aug: with ye Armes
Smith. & Browning impaled viz:
on a cheveron ingrailed between 6
crossles fitchee or 3 flourie de Lis
ye impalem: & 3 bars wavie arg: then
terly g & or a bend ar ye third al
cond ye 4 as ye first, & under writ

Ri St george clarenceux

hanc Geneologiam approbavit

Aug: Vincent
Windsor

um ... gnitum et in monumentis Collegij
raldorum tempore visitakonis
Gloucess: 1623 relatum

Jo Philipott RougeDragon

Harris of Cullorn in Wilts —
Mr Savage, wife of Tetbury.

This was ye Seal of Walt.
Savage great grandfather of
Mr Charles S. of Tetbury
when he was High Shir of
Worcestsh.

In the paper produced by Mr Webb
Grandfathers handwriting there ...

— At Thacham beyond New
the Armes of Webbe and Rich
upon the Tomb of Mr Fuller
directed to be sett there by Mr
George Herald.

The Webbs bury at North ...
Wiltshire — where 'tis suppose
are Mont: of the Webb —

Mr Stokes of Nonsha ...
a Pedegree on Parchment
his Descent is derived linea ...
Adam de Stokke qui ...
his wife temp: E. 2. 1312 ...
seised of the mannor of ...
Rushshall & Stokke in co ...
In which Pedegree ye Armes ...
In a ... double quer ...

for Mr Kingscott pond three ...
a draught of a Pedegree newly ...
from their Evidences as may be ...
ning with Arthur father of Mysch ...
temp: Cong: & ye Armes there par ...
Arg: 10 Escalops sable on a ...
a mullet pierced or

Mr Wyse, 3 Otters, field Arg

Pott by Rob: Cock Esq
by Rob: Webbe of Tiff ...
the Ancient Armes ...
I do find that his ...
and may bear lawfully ...
to say Sables 3 Escallo
a Crest sill. On a W ...
Arg: Mantled gules ...
Posterity. 1591. 1. ...
office, but ye Seal is ...

Mr Isinghons Armes 3 Spear

Gainsford.
Coshalton in ...
from whom he ...
ye Crest a Merm
holding a bunch of ...
ye right hand.
this Armis He beareth ...

(These Armes are painted
at ye Staton of Mr Daunts
Pedegree but not attested)

an old Genereall
a Scocheon
these Armes hilt.

Mr James produced

Winter of Dirham's
le —

Hodges of Shipton

Mr Clifford of Framptons
Armes

entertain at dinner all those who entered their arms and descents. But though gentlemen were thus summoned, Dugdale added that the heralds still 'ride to every knight's house and take notice there, as also to such esquires as will have them come'.

Between 1570 and his death in 1588 Robert Glover, Somerset Herald, visited several northern counties as deputy to his father in law William Flower, Norroy. Previous Visitation pedigree entries had consisted almost solely of narratives unsupported by evidence or even dates. But Glover initiated a great change and his last three Visitation books, those of Cheshire 1580, Staffordshire 1583 and Yorkshire 1584-5, include transcripts of charters from family muniments and other record extracts, both to prove particular pedigrees and for general interest (21). Glover was ahead of his time and had no equal until Augustine Vincent, Windsor Herald, who made Visitations as deputy to William Camden, Clarenceux, between 1618 and 1623.

The Visitations made between 1561 and 1635 had covered the whole country and much of it more than once, but, the troubles which led to the Civil War coming on, no more was then done under Charles I. In 1642 the king betook himself to Oxford, where most of the heralds joined him. John Beauchamp, Portcullis, a supporter of the Parliament, was left apparently in sole charge of the College of Arms in London. Three more of his colleagues later joined him there and in 1646 the Parliament (which rejected its king) appointed two Kings of Arms of its own, Edward Bysshe and Arthur Squibb, and promoted William Ryley, one of the king's heralds, to the third kingship. The heralds took part at Oliver Cromwell's second installation as Protector with augmented powers in 1657 and in the same year moves were made for a revival of Visitation. Cromwell, however, died in 1658 and Visitation was not in the event resumed until after Charles II's Restoration in 1660.

21 Page of a rough original Visitation book of Robert Glover, Somerset Herald, deputy to William Flower, Norroy King of Arms, of Yorkshire 1584–5. College of Arms MS. 2nd D5. f. 58, Pedigree of Darell of Sessay citing charter evidence.

Omnibus &c. Edmundus de Lacy Constabularius Cestrie Salutem. Noverit universitas vestra me confirmasse Deo et ecclesie Sancti Oswaldi de Nostle et Canonicis Regularibus eiusdem loci dimidiam carucatam terre, in qua sita est ecclesia eorundem Canonicorum super riuarium &c. Et liberam suam electionem ad Priores suos eligendos secundum tenorem rescripti meum et Canonicis Sancti Oswaldi de Nostle &c. Testibus Domino Hugone disfonlatre de Beth, Domino Ricardo Foliot, Domino Ada de Nouo Mercato, Domino Johanne de Bek, Domino Rado de Horbiry, Domino Johanne de Hodole, Domino Galfrido de Dutton et aliis.

Sigillum Edmundi de Lacy Constabularij Cestrie.

Quæ sequuntur ex chartis Johannis Daunay militis collectæ sunt. 1584:

Willelmus Darell de Sezay in com. Ebor, tempore Regis Johannis.

1270 — Willelmus Darell = Ada filia et heres Petri &c. opinatur.

Beatrix uxor Johannis Maulevercer de Aluerton sive Dalto, 1283 — Marmaducus Darell miles 28 E.1. = Heluisa filia Willelmi de Insula. Galfridus Darell. Willelmus de Holtby miles = Beatrix.

7 E.2 — Willelmus Darell miles 30 E.1 = Johanna filia Willelmi de Holtby miles 1283. xj E.1. Willelmus de Holtby xj E.2.

1358 — Marmaducus Darell miles senior = Cecilia 28 E.3. Johannes Darell 33 E.3 = Alicia uxor 33 E.3. Thomas 7 E.2. Alexander de Ledys = Elizabetha 1358.

Willelmus Darell miles 1354 = Elizabetha 29 E.3. Elizabetha filia et heres Alexandri de Ledys 33 E.3 vocat Marmaduc Darell auunc.

Johanna filia Willelmi Mewynson 1364 31 E.3 = Marmaducus junior Darell de Sezay 31 E.3 1364 = Alicia filia Ranulphi Pigot, soror Galfridi 44 E.3 uxor secunda Marmaduci. = Petrus de Rowthe secundus maritus. Willelmus Darell de Dalton 13 E.2. Johanna soror Petri de Dalton 14 E.2. Willelmus atte Welle de Dalton.

Thomas Darell forsan nothus 23 E.3. xj R.2 — Willelmus filius Marmaduci Darell 43 E.3. = Emma superstit anno xj R.2. Elizabetha. Willelmus filius Darell de Dalton = Agnes filia Willelmi atte Welle de Dalton que superstit 43 E.3. Emma 40 E.3.

Marmaducus Darell 14 R.2 = Johanna filia Johannis Bigod de Stevington militis 14 R.2. [3] Johannes Darell 14 R.2 de Calehill Kent. [2] Willelmus Darell de Wiltshire 20 14.6 14 R.2. [4] Henricus Darell 14 R.2. [5] Galfridus Darell 39 E.3. Alicia.

Edmundus Darell miles obijt 1438 = Isabella filia et heres Georgij Etton fratris iunioris Johannis Etton de Gillinge militis quæ obijt 2 idus Maij 1448.

Georgius Darell miles obijt 1466 5 cal. Aprilis. = Margareta filia Willelmi Plumpton militis obijt 1487 2 id. Maij. Johannes Darell miles obijt 1474 Non. Aprilis. = Johanna uxor 2 H.6. Radus Darell frater Georgij 18 H.7.

Johannes Darell miles obijt sine prole 7 H.7. = Catherina Skargays uxor. Thomas Darell frater et heres Johannis sine prole = Margeria uxor superstes 18 H.7. Marmaducus Darell sine prole. Guido Daunay miles = Johanna uxor et heres Thomæ Darell de Sezay 18 H.7.

Johannes Daunay miles

Thomas Daunay miles

Johannes Daunay miles uxor 1584

New Commissions were then issued in 1663. By 1670 eleven counties of the northern province had been visited and by 1677 eighteen of the southern. For those Visitations made in this series by the great William Dugdale, Norroy and afterwards Garter, we have not only the account in his diary and a note of the procedure which he wrote in old age, but also the lists, summonses, rough papers, drafts and correspondence, which, unlike his predecessors, he carefully preserved and handed over to the College. We have considerable records of this kind also for the last series of Visitations, of twelve counties of the southern province, between 1681 and 1687.

In Dugdale's and in these last twelve we not only find the procedure developed to a higher efficiency, but a greater detail of entry and a more critical scholarship in the pedigrees. On this subsequent practice at the College of Arms in tracing, examining and registering pedigrees has been founded. Thus the experience of Visitation over a century and a half or more had brought the English heralds – or some of them – from a romantic, amateur concern with genealogy to the first phase of modern genealogical scholarship. This may therefore be the moment to give some thought to the development of genealogy itself as a study and discipline.

5
ANCESTORS

HUMAN INTEREST IN ANCESTRY is a widespread, primitive thing, which some forms of social organization foster while others discourage and suppress it. Where a society is based on the family, so that property and rights and status depend on kinship and descent, genealogy must be important. But where this familial society yields to one in which the emphasis is on purely individual rights, where political, legal and economic relations are personal and not family affairs, there ancestry and kinship lose much of their importance, and interest in them may be thought foolish or old fashioned.

Familial society itself takes such different forms as the tribal and the feudal. Both these have their genealogies and genealogists, but of strongly contrasted kinds. Whereas tribal genealogies trace the whole kindred, feudal genealogies follow the lines of legal inheritance. In a tribal society genealogists may be bards, themselves often a hereditary class, who remember, with much else, everyone's ancestry and relationship. In the feudal society the general concern becomes narrowed to the genealogies of the ruling class, and those who owe hereditary service. When the feudal in its turn dissolves into the atomic, contractual society, the feudal associations give genealogists a bad name with the innovators, the advocates of reform or revolution. But this is a passing phase, for the deeper, tribal roots will eventually reassert themselves and genealogical addiction returns, as we see it doing now, on a populist tide.

This short account of a complex matter does scant justice to the multiplicity of human attitudes to ancestry. There is for instance the question of respect for truth. In all the phases there are some who want, whether for romantic or interested reasons, to glorify or at least improve – whether their own ancestry or that of others. At the other pole are those dull, literal minded fellows – like the present writer – who see no point in a pedigree unless they believe it true, or at the minimum think it possible that it may be true. But what are we to think of such a genuine scholar as Sir Egerton Brydges (d. 1837), who seems not merely to have forged or procured the forgery of parish register entries to support his claim to a peerage, but so much to have resented the rejection of that claim by the House of Lords that he undertook the vast labour of editing a valuable and scholarly nine volume peerage 'in order that a few of its pages might transmit a record of his family wrongs to posterity'. Or how shall we interpret that learned antiquary and friend of scholars, Sir Edward Dering (d. 1644) who, having invented for himself a Saxon pedigree, interpolated the name and arms of a fictitious ancestor into ancient rolls of arms which belonged to him and set up pseudo-ancestral brasses in Pluckley church? John Lord Lumley (d. 1609), with a pedigree genuinely proved from the twelfth century, felt it necessary to bring from Durham to the church of Chester-le-Street, where they remain, three effigies of mediaeval knights, supposed to be his ancestors but probably not so, and to complete the series with eleven new ones. Small wonder then, if his tales of his forefathers drew from King James I the comment 'I did na ken Adam's name was Lumley' (*EG* 359). One should, however, in this connection remember that both then and much later series of ancestral portraits were not uncommonly made up, sometimes by adding desired names or arms to existing portraits, sometimes by the painting of imaginary portraits, as with the formidable series of Scottish kings at Holyrood house.

In comparison with these exploits those of heralds and others who invented pedigrees for gain are simple and comprehensible. The culmination of this activity in England was in the reigns of Elizabeth I and James I, when the genuine scholars of the first great age of such scholarship were competing with ever more desperate fabricators for the patronage of pedigree enthusiasts. J. Horace Round (1854-1928), the great critical genealogist, distinguished four kinds of spurious pedigree, 'those that rested on garbled versions of perfectly genuine documents, such as Philpot the herald was an adept at constructing, those which rested on alleged transcripts of wholly imaginary documents, those which rested on actual forgeries expressly concocted for the purpose, and lastly those which rested on nothing but sheer fantastic fiction' (*RFO* pp. 270-1). Round might have added a fifth class, more and more favoured as criticism has disposed of the others, that of pedigrees which rest on a strained and unlikely, but not always demonstrably impossible, interpretation of genuine evidence.

Round, of course, was thinking only of pedigrees based on documentary evidence. He was no believer in traditional pedigrees and in the context he was dealing with was right, for when the kind of genealogist Round was writing of gives 'tradition' as his authority for a statement, he is likely to be propounding a figment of imagination. But in tribal societies oral tradition has really existed – indeed exists – though it is by no means always reliable. Indeed it gives the fabulist its own special opportunities of attaching fictitious to genuine traditions.

The English heralds encountered traditional genealogy in Wales. Dugdale about 1680 refers to the Kings of Arms' early custom of 'going to the houses of the chiefs of families where they took notice of their marriages and issue with their arms, as the Bards did heretofore in Wales, and of late time if not still in those parts'. The heralds had direct knowledge of this because their ignorance of the Welsh language compelled them to make Visitations in Wales entirely through Welsh deputies. The first of these, Griffith Hiraethog, who died in 1566, was in fact a bard and the pedigrees written down by him and his successors were almost exclusively traditional, orally transmitted genealogies. The work of the present Wales Herald Extraordinary, Major Francis Jones, has done much to establish the veracity of many of the traditions, while exposing the special forms of error which could creep in. Generations might drop out or be reduplicated. The first ancestor in a genuine tradition might be attached to an older line in which he really had no place while the oldest lines of all, those of kings and princes, might be extended backwards to link with classical or biblical pedigrees.

The critical study of genealogy which by degrees sorted out the wheat from the chaff began effectively in the sixteenth century though the effort to base pedigrees and history generally on reliable evidence goes back further. When John Rous wrote, drew and painted his roll of the Earls of Warwick about 1480 (Plate IV), he made shift, in Oswald Barron's words 'to dress up the ancienter knights of his roll in the chain mail which he had seen upon tombs that were old when he was young'. Rous thus attempted archaeology, yet sixteenth and seventeenth century herald painters would head their pedigree rolls with fanciful ancestral portraits of Saxon thanes or Norman knights in Renaissance versions of Roman armour or plumed theatrical fancy dress.

William Bowyer, Keeper of the Records in the Tower of London, comprising Domesday Book (1086-7) and the Chancery and Exchequer Rolls from the twelfth century onwards, was using these for genealogy in the 1560s. He thus worked out a pedigree for Lord Treasurer Winchester who in 1567 wrote to Cecil that he had desired Leicester to show this to him and to the Queen 'that his service may be known, whereof will grow great reformation amongst the heralds, that maketh their books at a venture and not by the records' (Professor R. B. Wernham, *EHS* pp. 17-18, quoting *State Papers, Domestic, Elizabeth*, No. xlii, f. 101). Reformation indeed so grew that Professor D. C. Douglas said of the *Baronage of England* (1675-6) by Sir William Dugdale, Garter King of Arms, that no single work has ever done so much for the history of the English aristocracy (*DCD* pp. 52-3).

In the pedigrees in this book and in *The Antiquities of Warwickshire* (1656) Dugdale was perhaps the first English historian to carry out, so far as he could, the great historical principle of quoting a contemporary record for every statement made. This, of course, was only possible where records existed and their existence for the families on which Dugdale was working was solely due to feudal and Norman legalism and administrative efficiency. Their genealogical value and reliability derive essentially from their original practical intention leaving the minimum of room for misunderstanding or fraud. They relate first to the feudal lords and knights but more and more as time went on to the legal appearances of lesser men.

Almost at the same time as the Visitations began a penultimate step to total comprehensiveness was taken when parish registers of baptism, marriage and burial were inaugurated by Thomas Cromwell in 1538. An early instance of their genealogical use is in the pedigree (22) worked out before 1699 for Sir Comport Fitch by Samuel Stebbing, assistant to Gregory King from about 1683, Rouge Rose 1698 and Somerset Herald 1700-19 (*EG* 375-6). But even were parish registers complete – and there are huge gaps in them, especially in their first century or so – they could not cover those dissenters who would not be baptized or even married or buried by the Church of England. In 1747 the heralds, aware of the genealogical gap this left, authorized two of their number to enter into discussion with the heads of the Dissenters and Jews about setting up a civil register of births, deaths and marriages at the College of Arms (23). This was agreed to and in 1748 set up, but unhappily was so little used that the surviving record books are chiefly interesting as showing the way the wind was blowing.

General compulsory civil registration _under Act of Parliament came in at length in 1837 and the oldest English census returns which have been preserved date from 1841. So just as by about 1700 parish registers had existed long enough to be of real value to genealogists and to make the tracing of pedigrees possible for a whole new range of families, so in the 1970s there is a reasonable hope of tracing any English man or woman four or five generations back at least. Before that the problems grow but the vast, if imperfect, bulk of record still makes it certain that, if they could be tackled comprehensively, enormous numbers of pedigrees of families in all stations of life could be traced back for centuries – as many have been.

A young man or woman living now may have as many as thirty or forty ancestors of about the fifth generation back, living in 1837 and traceable through the General Register.

22 Evidence for the pedigree of Sir Comport Fitch, Baronet, collected 1699 by Samuel Stebbing, Rouge Rose, and recorded in College of Arms Reg. 3D14 ff. 7[b] and 8, with the pedigree. (*See overleaf.*)

I Richard Fitch of Stoke by Clare in the County of Suffolk aged Fifty Nine Years o
thereabouts, son of Joshua Fitch of Hare Street Hall in Birdbroke in Com. Essex, who wa
son of Ralph Fitch of Coots in Bumsted, which Ralph was Son of Richard Fitch of Ma
hall in Stoke aforesaid, descended of the Family of Fitch of Bumsted, do hereby Certify
that I have very often heard, both my Father and several of my near Relations affir
that the Fitches of Coots and Welden, were Originally Descended and Sprung from th
Fitches of Brasenhead in the Parish of Lyndsell in the County of Essex; and that y sai
Fitches of Coots and Welden, had and lived in the Reputation of Gentlemen, and did
bear and use a Coat of Arms as Gentlemen, which were three Leopards heads between a
Chevron, and a Leopard for their Crest; And I do further Certify that I Personally ve
well knew Mr. Richard Fitch of Coots, who was an Attorney at Law, and Father to sai
Thomas Fitch the last Owner of Coots, and of Pennington Fitch, which Richard died
about 30 Years past; That the said Thomas was a Captain of Horse in the Service of
King Charles the first, and died about the Year 1675. and left Issue one only son w
died Unmarried within a few Years after him; And that Pennington Fitch afore
died in London, but left no Issue to the best of my Remembrance, And I do likewi
Certify that I have often heard my sd Father and Relations say, that some of the
Fitches of Bumsted, did remove from thence into Hertfordshire, but it was before
my Memory, In Witness whereof I have hereunto set my hand and seal at Steeple
Bumsted aforesaid this third day of February 1699.

Memorandum upon the Question put to
the said Richard Fitch, by William
Fytche of Woddham Walter in Essex
Esq. whether he ever heard of y Fitches
of Garnets, or Woodham Walter, he
declard that he never did hear that
the Fitches of Bumsted were related
to those other Branches.

Signd   Richard Fitch

This Certificate was Signd and
Seald after the Memorandum
first made in the Presence of me.

Signd   Samll. Thompson

An Acco.t of the Christnings and burials of the Fitches Extracted from the Ch
Register of the Parish of Barkway in the County of Hertford 1.Decr. 1699.

Thomas Fitche son of John Fytche, was baptizd the xxiiijth day of July 1586.
Felix Fiche son of John Fyche, was baptizd the xijth day of April 1588.
John Fitche son of John Fytche, was baptized the first day of July 1593.
Grace Fitche the daur of John Fitch, baptized the 12 day of October 1594.
Elizabeth Fitche the daur of John Fitche, baptizd the 5th day of November 1598.
William Fiche the Son of John Fyche, was baptizd the 8th day of April Ano. 1604:
John the Son of William Fitch and Alice his Wife, baptized Janry 1.1635.
John the Son of William Fitch and Alice his Wife, buried June the 24.1636.
Thomas the Son of William Fitch Jenr. and Alice his Wife, baptizd Decr.17.1637.

John

John the Son of William Fitch Sen. and Alice his Wife baptized Febr. 2. 1642.
John Fitch buried 14 January 1630.
Allice Fych buried the 7.th day of December 1648.

Mr Holdsworth Certificate of the aforesaid Christnings and Burials.

1. Decr 1699. The Accompt of Baptisms and Burials enter'd on the other side was Extracted out
of the Register Book of the Parish of Barkway in the County of Hartford in ye Presence of the Vicar of the said Parish, In Witness whereof and also that it is a true
Draught, I hereunto set my hand the day and year above Written.

Signd Jude Holdsworth Vicar of Barkway.

John the Son of John Fytch of Welden baptized the ij.^d of Februarye 1561.

2 Decr 1699. This Acco.^t of the Baptizing of John Fitch the Son of John Fitch of Welden was Extracted from the Church Reg.^r
of the Parish of Steeple Bumpsted in the County of Essex in the Presence of
Matthew Relton Clark of Bumsted.

An Extract from the Church Register of little Canfield in the County of Essex of the
Baptisms, Marriages and Burials of the Fytches in that Parish, as also the Copies
of two Inscriptions on Gravestones in the Chancel of the said Church taken at Canfield aforesaid 2 Febry 1699.

Baptism

Francys son of William Fytche Gent.^e baptiz'd 5 Septr 1563.

Marriage

George Fytch and Joan Thurgood married 14 September 1574

Burials

William Fytche the Son of William Fytch Gent.^e buried 5 Novr 1571.
William Fytch the Son of William Fytch Gent.^e buried 22 Decr 1578.

On a Flat Stone on the South side of the Chancel in little Canfield Church
are the Figures of a Man between his two Wives in Brass Plates, and just
over their heads a large Plain Scocheon with the Single Arms of Fytch Sil.^t
a Cheveron between three Leopards heads with a Crese.^t for Difference, and
under the Inscription, on the right side the figures of five Children, and
on the left side of four Children, with four Smaller Scocheons at ye Corners
of the Stone, of the Arms aforesaid.

The Inscription on a Plate of Brass

Here lyethe buryed under this Stone the Boddie of William Fytche Esquire late Lord
of this Towne, who had two Wyffes Elizabeth and Anne, and the said William
had Yssue by Elizabeth his first Wife two Sonnes and three Daughters, and by
Anne his Second Wyfe four Sonnes, and the said William being of the Age of 82
Years chang'd this Lyfe the 20.th of December in Anno Domini 1578.

5.

N.º 15.
Jacob de Mattos

My Son Jacob, by Rebecca my Wife, Daughter of Abraham Mocatta of St. Andrews Undershaft in the City of London, to whom I was married at the abovementioned Parish Church on the 2nd Day of December 1730 was borne at my House in the above written Parish on the 9th Day of January 1731/2 Witness my Hand this 18th May 1748

Witnesses present at the Birth)
gracia Mocatta
gracia ximenes

Moses de mattos Son of Jacob de mattos by Sarra de Daughter of David Brabo

Signed in the } Jas. Lane Richm.
Presence of } Thos. Thornbory) Windsor

N.º 16.
Abraham de Mattos

My Son Abraham by Rebecca my said Wife, was born at my House aforesaid on the 9th Day of January 1733/4 Witness my Hand this 18th May 1748

Witnesses present at the Birth.
gracia Mocatta
gracia ximenes

Moses de mattos

Signed in the } Jas. Lane Richmond
Presence of } Thos. Thornbory) Windsor

N.º 17.
Grace de Mattos

My Daughter Grace by Rebecca my said Wife, was born at my House aforesaid, on the 29th Day of September 1735. Witness my Hand this 18th May 1748.

Witnesses present at the Birth)
gracia Mocatta
gracia ximenes

Moses de mattos

Signed in the } Jas. Lane Richmond
presence of } Thos. Thornbory) Windsor

23 The Heralds' Register of Births, Volume A. No. 1, page 5. Opened in 1747 (see p. 45). This page shows entries of some well known Jewish families. *HCEC* Nos. 123; *HE* 381-3.

This, of course, is on all lines – two parents, four grandparents and so forth. I do not mean that such tracing back in the General Register is always simple or even possible. With common names, for instance, there can be difficult problems of identity between persons of the same name. There is, however, a fair chance of completeness or some approach to it at this point. At the next stage, however, we have a different problem. There is no longer a central source with a single index. Instead there is a great number of local and special sources, which cannot, however, help us till we know which of them to look in.

If the man we are seeking had a name as common as John Smith and we only know that he was born in London, the chances of getting further may be slim. But if he came from a small village or had a rare, localized name they will be vastly better. There are in my view four factors which mainly govern the chances of success in tracing English pedigrees: status, record, name and continuity. Status may seem obvious. A nobleman is almost by definition a man with a pedigree; but nobility is not the only kind of status. Eminence is relative and can be purely local; can attach to wealth, office, political activity, vocational skill, and even to the bad eminence of criminality. Any of these things may focus on men or families that kind of concern which causes track to be kept of them and record made. That brings us to the second factor, record; and it is evident that for genealogists the preservation or loss and the availability of relevant record is and always must be a crucial factor. The fire which destroyed the Four Courts in Dublin in 1922 and the bomb which fell on the Exeter Probate Registry in 1942, have reduced the possibilities for Irish and Devon genealogy beyond calculation. The genealogist has to know what records exist and where and how to use them and get from them the last drop of evidence on his problems.

This ties up with the knowledge he needs to have of the other factors. Records have their roots in social history because they were made to serve practical purposes. Records of feudal tenure give place to records of property and taxation. To evaluate the evidence of legal records some knowledge is needed of the legal background, and so with others. The connection of heralds with economic history may not seem obvious but they were at its birth in the person of Gregory King (1648-1712), Rouge Dragon 1677 and Lancaster Herald 1689. He lies buried in St Benet Paul's Wharf, the Wren church opposite the College of Arms where the heralds had their pew. His epitaph there tells us that 'He was a skilful herald, a good accomptant, surveyor and mathematician, a curious penman, and well versed in political arithmetick'. He was one of the fathers of demography and his calculation of the population of England in 1695 (partly from the same books which provided the Visitation summons lists) was perhaps the first which can be considered reasonably accurate. His assessment of social facts in relation to the practical business of heraldic Visitation is thus of interest. In 1682, as deputy to Sir Henry St George, Clarenceux, for the Visitation of Warwickshire, he wrote when compiling the summons list, 'I do not think there are any persons left out worth summoning or at least very few, but I believe there is not a third part if so many that are really gentlemen'. The heralds had to assess gentility and the Court of Chivalry at times to decide it on social criteria. In France a nobleman who engaged in trade might lose his nobility (and the tax exemption which went with it) by *dérogeance,* but the English Court of Chivalry was told in 1634 that 'many citizens of great worth and esteem descended of very ancient gentle families' were soap boilers by trade and still accounted gentlemen.

In England, in fact, since the Norman Conquest if not earlier the confusion of classes has been such that it has been hard to find clear and sharp lines between them anywhere. This may not have made transit up or down from one to another easier, but it has meant that when such transit has taken place it could be accepted with less fuss. Witness the grants of arms to new men under Elizabeth I which scandalized the conservative, as when a grant was made in 1596 to the father of one William Shakespeare. It is, I believe, this relative ease of social transition which has led at times to concentration on small social distinctions and what has seemed at times to foreigners an English obsession with social class – not, as some have thought, social rigidity but quite the contrary. The survival of the House of Lords, reluctant and less reluctant Life Peers and all, is evidence rather of an almost overstrained elasticity.

For the genealogist this English social fluidity and gently sloping social profile mean that paupers can trace descent from kings and noblemen from labourers much more often than those who have not studied the matter might expect. The sixty four great-great-great-great-grandparents of Queen Elizabeth the Queen Mother exemplify one aspect of this:

two dukes, a duke's daughter, the daughter of a marquess, three earls, an earl's daughter, a viscount, a baron, some half dozen country gentlemen, an East India Company director, a provincial banker, two bishops' daughters, three clergymen (one born in America), a Huguenot refugee's daughter, an Irish officer of Jacobite descent in the French service and his French mistress, the landlord of an inn, a London toyman and a London plumber.

The reverse process of social descent can be seen where whole progenies are traced, though less easily and often. The origins of families which have come up in the world are studied both by their members and by others, while the fate of those who sink is often both obscure in itself and likelier to be left so. However, general trends and incidental discoveries alike point to the frequency of the fact of such descent (*EG* pp. 207-22, 238-9).

We must look again in this connection at another of our four factors making for success or failure in tracing ancestry – that of name. Rarity of surname (or indeed of forename) is a social accident if ever there was one. Fentiman is very rare, Howard rather common. But the genealogist's concern is not just with numerical frequency but also with the probability or otherwise of different families being of the same ultimate stock. In some cases it has been shown to be highly probable that all or most bearers were of one kin. This is likely though not sure to be so where a family name comes from that of a knight who took his from a rare or unique place name in Normandy, as Champernowne from Cambernon, or Chaworth from Sourches, or Mynors from Minières. The same may be true of a villein or yeoman family named from an English place of origin, perhaps a hamlet or farmstead so small as to give a name to only one family and happening itself to have a rare name, such as Armitage or Ormondroyd (*RYWR*). It can happen, perhaps, even with a rare occupational surname like Pilcher.

The study of these patterns, though much advanced lately, mainly through the Marc Fitch English Surname project, is still only in its early stages and we are still learning step by step from particular traceable instances what the patterns may have been in other cases.

6

THE COLLEGE OF ARMS

IN THE FOURTEENTH and fifteenth centuries the heralds of Western Europe thought of themselves as an international brotherhood, *Le Noble Office d'Armes* (Plate VII). Their concern with tournaments and employment as messengers on several levels up to that of diplomacy promoted this feeling and made common standards and conventions highly desirable, and these in fact were the conventions of chivalry. At the battle of Agincourt the French and English heralds stood together at their post of observation keeping count of the lords and knights who were killed. After it was over the English heralds stayed with their masters and the French departed whither they would.

To settle their affairs the heralds from time to time held meetings or Chapters and this led on to incorporation, formal or informal. In 1407 the French heralds won the use of a chapel in the Royal palace in Paris. In 1415 Henry V of England created the new office of Garter King of Arms (Plate VIII), linked with the Order of the Garter and with authority over other English heralds, of whom by this time a number existed with territorial or heraldic names of office, some in the service of the Crown and others in that of noblemen.

In 1420 the heralds of the English Crown held a Chapter and resolved to adopt a common seal, but they received no charter of incorporation till 1484 when Richard III granted them this together with a great house, Coldharbour by the Thames in London, there to keep their records and 'to have therein their studies and learnings'. But the very next year King Henry VII came in, King Richard lost his crown and his life, and the heralds lost Coldharbour and had no corporate home till Queen Mary gave them a fresh charter and the site of the present College of Arms, with the old mansion there called Derby Place, in 1555.

Neither the 1484 charter, nor its loss, nor the 1555 charter changed the status of the heralds as a department of the Royal Household, which till 1521 was under the Constable and the Marshal, and from that date, when the Constable disappeared, under the Marshal, or Earl Marshal, solely. As a corporation the College possesses its home and keeps the records. As servants of the Sovereign the heralds prepare, conduct and take part in ceremonies, the Kings of Arms grant arms and they and their colleagues carry out researches, trace, compile and record pedigrees and perform such kindred duties as from time to time may be asked of them.

The old College building was destroyed in the Great Fire of London in 1666, but the records were saved and taken, presumably by water, to Westminster. In January 1666/7 a notice appeared in the *Gazette* that the Heralds' Office was kept in a room in the Palace of Westminster, near the Court of Requests, formerly called the Queen's Court, and there it remained till 1674. In the interval money had been raised, not without difficulty, from the subscriptions of the nobility and gentry and the profits of the Duke of Albemarle's funeral in 1670 (see p. 84). This enabled the central block on the old site to be built and occupied in 1674. By 1677, however, building was at a standstill for want of funds, but Sir William Dugdale, just made Garter, built the north-west corner and in 1680 Sir Henry St George, Clarenceux, gave the profits of Visitation of six counties, so that the north and west sides were finished by 1683. The work was carried out under the supervision of Francis Sandford (Rouge Dragon 1661, Lancaster herald 1675-89) by Morris Emott or Emmett, Master Bricklayer in the Office of Works from 1677, who worked for Wren at Chelsea, Windsor, Kensington and Hampton Court. His brother William, woodcarver to the King, also played an important part in the rebuilding. The Emmett pedigree was entered at the Visitation of London in 1687.

In that year the east and south sides being still mostly unbuilt a 61-year building lease for their completion, uniform with the rest, was granted to Ephraim Beacham, a stone-cutter who worked for Wren at St Paul's. The three houses which he built came into the heralds' hands in 1748. They were then let out on short leases, sometimes to heralds, till 1866, when the construction of Queen Victoria Street led to the curtailment of the south side and the reabsorption of

53

these houses to make good the lost space. This and the construction of a new Record Room on the north side in 1842-3, completed the building as it now is apart from the fine iron gates and railings on the south side (Plate XIII). These, which were made for Goodrich Court, Herefordshire, in the 1870s or 1880s, were given to the College in 1956 by an American benefactor, Mr Blevins Davis, to replace the Victorian ones requisitioned for war purposes in 1942. In August 1939 the Records were removed for safety to Thornbury Castle, Gloucestershire, the home of Sir Algar Howard, then Norroy, later Garter. Six years later they returned. On the night of 10-11 May 1941 the College building had a narrow escape when a fire raid destroyed all the buildings to the east of it as far as the tower of St Mildred's, Bread Street.

Though the building thus just escaped all but minor war damage, the roof and much of the brickwork were found after the war to be in a parlous condition, partly through shaking, partly through unavoidable neglect. By 1954 the choice had to be made between abandoning it and spending on its repair far more than the College had. The second choice was made possible by generous public subscription and a matching government grant. In 1956 a charitable trust, entitled *The College of Arms Trust* was set up, for the maintenance and embellishment of the College building, the establishment of a museum where the College treasures might be seen, and for other charitable purposes connected with the College. Great efforts have been and at the time of writing are being made to bring the Museum plan to fruition.

Before the heralds acquired Derby Place, their working books might pass precariously to successors by individual arrangement, but might also sometimes be sold by widows or families to collectors. Other manuscript books again they had produced in the first place for noblemen and other clients. Of such heralds' books outside the College some remain in private hands, but by far the largest single collection has been brought together over a long period, and through many channels, in the Department of Manuscripts, formerly of the British Museum, now of the British Library.

One example will suffice to show how an old collection

may become dispersed and the clues to its nature lost until its scattered elements are located and compared. Henry VIII's Garter King of Arms (1505-34), Sir Thomas Wriothesley, was both a collector and producer of heraldic manuscripts on a large scale, as on a lesser scale his father John Writhe (Garter 1478-1504) had been. Wriothesley built himself a great house, called Garter House, in Red Cross Street adjoining Barbican House in the parish of St Giles, Cripplegate, and in the top of it a chapel called *Sanctae Trinitatis in Alto*. Here presumably his scriveners and herald painters, whose several hands can be clearly distinguished, did their work for him.

One of his greatest undertakings was evidently planned as a complete pictorial digest of English arms down to his own day, arranged both as an Armory (that is, alphabetically) and as an Ordinary (that is, by form of design). Sections of the former are now contained in three separate volumes in the College of Arms, one in the British Library and one at the Society of Antiquaries, and of the latter in all but one of these. So it is with much else of this and earlier dates (*ASP* II. 258-9).

In 1568, four years after the heralds had moved into Derby Place, the Earl Marshal, Thomas Duke of Norfolk, issued *Orders to be observed and kept by the Officers of Arms* with special reference to the organization of their new home and of their work in it. These deal with the allocation of accommodation between the several officers and the library or office and with the custody and care of the records. This includes the institution of a system, which still in modified form continues, of 'waiting', by officers in rotation. During their turns on duty they must 'do their duty . . . to answer all such as shall have to do in the said office', and must deal in specified ways with searches, with fees paid, with certified extracts, entries in the records and so forth. Visitations, grants of arms, the conduct of funerals and Chapter meetings are also dealt with.

The scope of the heralds' duties at this date is indicated: first, the duties which have since bulked largest, 'the bearing, using, placing or quartering of any arms', and dealing with descents or pedigrees; secondly, 'the right usage and ceremonies to be observed at coronations, creations, funerals and all other such like solemnities and assemblies of honour and worthiness'; and thirdly the mediaeval duties by then becoming antiquated, 'the laws and orders of the field, the summoning of towns and holds, the taking, using and ransoming of prisoners, the taking of messages, the giving of defiances, the proclaiming or uttering of anything that may be given them in charge to declare, utter, pronounce or do to any foreign potentate, as also the receiving, entertaining, placing and serving of ambassadors or any other foreign estate'.

The year after issuing these orders Duke Thomas was committed to the Tower on suspicion of treason and in 1572 was found guilty and beheaded and his honours were forfeited. But his Orders of 1568, despite a period of some confusion, continued to govern the heralds. His grandson, Thomas Earl of Arundel, was made Earl Marshal again in 1621. His grandson in, turn, was restored to the Dukedom of Norfolk in 1660, and the present Duke of Norfolk and Earl Marshal, twelfth in male descent from the Duke attainted in 1572, still nominates the heralds for appointment by the Queen and still directs their activities.

VIII William Bruges, Chester herald 1398, Guienne King of Arms 1413, first Garter King of Arms 1415, died 1450; here shown kneeling before Saint George in the book in which, about 1430, he recorded the Founder Knights of the Garter, wearing their arms, with those of their successors to his day. He wears his tabard of the royal arms and a crown decorated with little shields probably designed to show the arms of Knights of the Garter, in Chaucer's words 'crounes wroght ful of lozenges' (p. 9). British Library MS Stowe 594. f. 5b; *CEMRA* 83.

VIII

IX

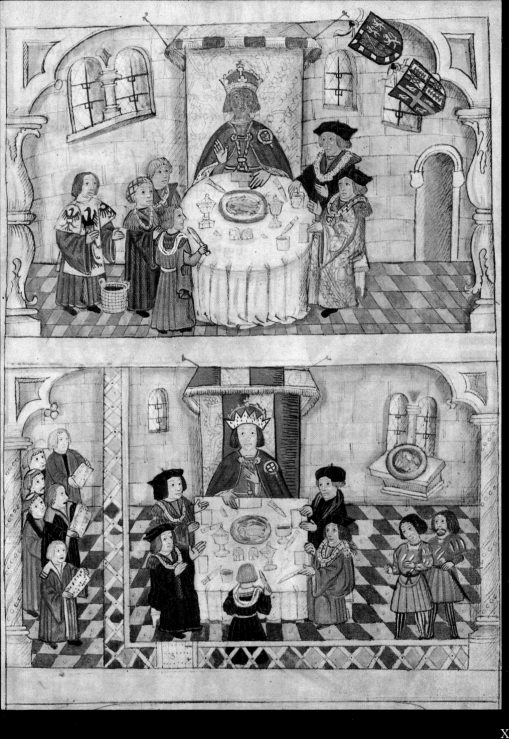

X

William Graham
Arch-Bish of Canterbury

Edward Stafford
Duke of Buckingham

XI

V
II
Va ▶
7b ▶

IX Shields, crests and badges of Yorkshire lords, part of a series of Yorkshire lords and gentry, recorded c. 1483 by William Ballard, March King of Arms, in a volume (College of Arms MS. M. 3 f. 53) which was bought from his widow after his death in 1490 by John Writhe, Garter King of Arms 1478-1504. In the top row the shield of Thomas Howard, created Earl of Surrey 1483, is painted out because of his attainder in 1485. He was, however, restored in 1489 and after his victory over the Scots at Flodden in 1513 was in 1514 created Duke of Norfolk. Among the badges are the Percy crescent, the Howard white lion, the Scrope chough and crab and the Clifford annulet. *CEMRA* 112.

X Paintings made for Sir Thomas Wriothesley, Garter 1504-34, in College of Arms MS. Vincent 152 (Prince Arthur's book) f. 178: (a) of Maximilian, King of the Romans (later Emperor) sitting at dinner on 12 September 1490, the day of his investiture with the Order of the Garter, with Sir Charles Somerset and John Writhe, Garter (father of Sir Thomas Wriothesley), who were sent to invest him. (b) Ferdinand, Archduke of Austria (later Emperor), grandson of Maximilian, sitting at dinner at Nuremberg on 8 December 1523, the day of his investiture with the Order of the Garter, with Lord Morley and Sir William Hussey on his right and Dr Edward Lee, Archdeacon of Colchester, and Sir Thomas Wriothesley, Garter, on his left, who were sent to invest him. Sixty four such Garter missions are recorded between 1470 and 1929. *CP.* Vol. II, App. B, p. 582 says that, 'In these missions the splendid formality, attending the investiture, has enhanced the value of that "most noble" Order, above all others, in the eyes of European Sovereigns'. The Garter Kings of Arms received notable rewards on these occasions. Some foreign sovereigns, however, came to England to be invested and installed and of late this has been usual.

XI Figures from the roll at Trinity College, Cambridge, painted for Sir Thomas Wriothesley, Garter 1504-34, of the procession to the Parliament of 1512: the Archbishop of Canterbury: Garter Wriothesley holding the roll of peers: Edward Stafford, Duke of Buckingham (d. 1521), carrying the Cap of Maintenance; Henry Stafford, his son (d. 1566), with the Sword of State: Henry VIII, not yet bearded, under a canopy. *PW* Pl. XVIII, pp. 549-50. *HE* Pl. XIV.

XII Drawing by Joseph Highmore, one of a series representing the Procession and Ceremonies of the Installation of the Knights of the Bath on 17 June 1725 at the institution of the Order. The Knights at dinner, Bath King of Arms, attended by heralds and pursuivants, proclaiming the style of Prince William, Duke of Cumberland (aged four), at the bringing in of the second course. *HE* Pl. XXXIV. The property of the National Trust, now at the Fitzwilliam Museum, Cambridge.

XIII   Watercolour drawing of the College of Arms from Queen Victoria Street, by Kamil Kubik about 1965.

XIV   Painted triptych, in carved and architectural frame in the church of Lydiard Tregoze, Wiltshire; first set up in 1615 by Sir John St John, Baronet (d. 1648), to commemorate his parents and ancestors, and later added to by him and by his successors down to the early eighteenth century. Four panels painted with pedigrees (including one of the 32 ancestors of the celebrated Henry St John (1678-1751), created Viscount Bolingbroke) open to reveal paintings of the persons commemorated. The original heraldic and genealogical material was furnished by Sir Richard St George, Clarenceux King of Arms (d. 1635), husband of Elizabeth, sister of Sir John St John, and later material probably by one or more of their descendants, Sir Henry St George, Garter (d. 1644), Sir Thomas St George, Garter (d. 1703) and Sir Henry St George, Garter (d. 1715). Sir Richard also probably gave help with the St John ancestral heraldry in the east window of the church of Battersea, Surrey (now London).

XV   College of Arms MS. I. 1, 'The Book of Monuments, 1619', was instituted in compliance with an order made 10 November 1618 by the Lords Commissioners for the Office of Earl Marshal in order to protect the heralds' conduct of funerals and in that connection to restrain 'the sinister practice of certain mechanical tradesmen, as painters, glasiers, stonecutters, carvers, and many other artificers, trading in armory, who presuming, without authority, to meddle with the marshalling of arms, the erecting of monuments, whereon armes are to be fixed' are forbidden to paint arms without the allowance and approbation of the Kings of Arms, or to set up arms on any monument, without it first be seen and allowed by the Kings and Officers of Arms whom it doth concern, the copy whereof with the form of the monument, to be drawn and entered into a book, which book shall be called The Book of Monuments, and shall be kept in the Office of Arms for ever'.

Only one carver seems in fact to have entered his designs, but this was Maximilian Colt, the King's Carver. His design here shown is for the hearse of Anne of Denmark, Queen of James I, 1619. The shields, guidons and banners on the canopy display the arms and badges of England, Scotland and Denmark; beneath it is the Queen's effigy in wax; on the four columns are the English, Scottish and Danish supporters. *HCEC* 127, 128; *HE* 239.

7
CEREMONIES

THE HERALDS' CONCERN with state ceremonial seems to derive both from their ceremonious duties at tournaments and from their subordination to the Constable and Marshal, who themselves had responsibilities in that field. Evidence before 1400 is scanty, merely establishing the presence of heralds on great occasions, but Nicholas Upton about 1440 says that 'heralds wear their coats of their masters' arms at their feasts and weddings, at Kings' and Queens' coronations and at ceremonies of princes, dukes and other great lords'. These coats of their masters' arms were already the heralds' distinctive wear in the thirteenth century and it seems that in early times heralds might wear their masters' own cast off coats. After 1500, when kings, lords and knights ceased to wear coats of their arms, the heralds still continued to do so and their tabards thus became distinctive survivals, like judges' wigs and bishops' gaiters at later dates.

The pursuivants, or junior heralds, wore their tabards 'athwart' with the sleeves at back and front and the longer parts as sleeves (24). The best tabards in the fifteenth century, and doubtless earlier, were already expensive because richly embroidered and of costly materials (25), whereas cheaper ones were painted. By Henry VIII's reign the tabards of the kings of arms were of satin or velvet, those of the heralds of damask and the pursuivants of sarsenet. For James I's coronation each king of arms had a tabard 'wrought on velvet with fine Venice gold', each herald and each pursuivant one 'painted with fine gold in oil upon damask'. By 1634 the heralds' and pursuivants' tabards also were embroidered and so they have continued.

24 Sir Peter Lely, drawing of a pursuivant. One of a series of drawings by Lely of figures from a Garter procession, probably of the 1670s. The pursuivant still wears his tabard athwart in the mediaeval way. Victoria and Albert Museum. *HE* Plates XXIV-XXIX (Pl. XXIX).

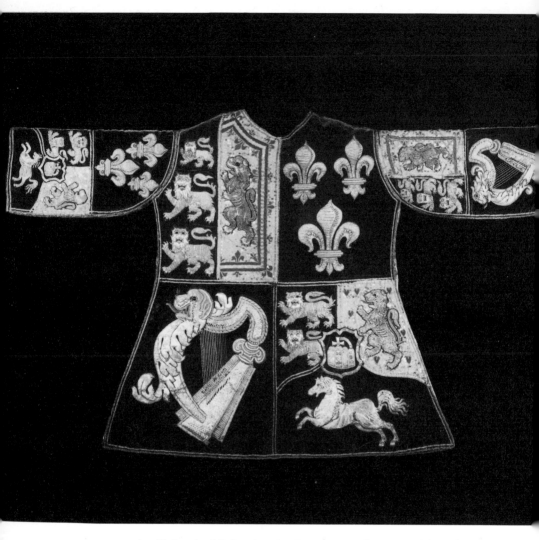

25 Tabard of John Anstis the younger (1708-54, joint Garter
with his father 1727, sole Garter 1744) as Blanc Coursier herald
(1726) and Principal Companion of the Order of the Bath (see
Plate XII), of the Royal Arms with the Duke's label of three
points argent the middle point charged with a St George's Cross.
This and his father's tabard, crown, sceptre, chain and badges
were, through the author, acquired in 1937 by the Victoria and
Albert Museum from Mrs Blanche Ker, a descendant of the
Anstis family.

The heralds of noblemen wore coats of their masters' arms. After the battle of Chatillon in 1453, where the great John Talbot, Earl of Shrewsbury, was killed, his mangled body was recognized by Shrewsbury his herald, who with tears trickling down his face threw his own coat of arms over his master's body. A painting of this Earl wearing his coat of arms exists in more than one version. One of them hung on a pillar over his widow's tomb in Old St Paul's. It is supposed to have been saved from the flames by one of the heralds at the time of the Great Fire of London and now hangs in the Earl Marshal's Court at the College of Arms.

Heralds themselves were ceremonially created, when they took an oath and their masters put their tabards on them and baptized them by their names of office with wine or water from a cup (sometimes of gold or silver) which should then be given them. In France the wine might be of the master's vineyard. Kings of Arms were also crowned and given rods or sceptres of a special form. Chaucer, whose wife seems to have been a daughter of Guienne King of Arms, wrote in 1383 of 'pursevauntes and heraudes', crying 'Largess' (as heralds did) and with a bowl for collecting it in which they 'shoken nobles and sterlinges'.

> 'and every man
> Of hem, as I yow tellen can,
> Had on him throwen a vesture,
> Which that men clepe a cote-armure,
> Embrowded wonderliche riche.'

And among them 'somme crouned were as kinges, With crounes wroght ful of losenges'. This probably means that the crowns were themselves decorated with little shields to

26 Pen drawing *c*. 1559 of the order of proceeding of Queen Elizabeth I to Westminster, College of Arms MS. M6. f. 416. (see 16, above): said to be 'procyding to a parliament or coronacion' and inferred by Stephen Martin Leake, Garter (MS. Ceremonials: 2. p. 357) to be for the proceeding from the Tower to Westminster 14 January 1558/9, the day before the coronation. However the Queen is here depicted *crowned*, so that the picture must be a composite one. The name of the Queen's Almoner, Dr Byll (f. 92) dates it before his death in 1561. *HCEC* No. 86. Pl. XII. (*See overleaf.*)

The gent pencionars on foote withe pollapes in their handes barehed

The Quieres and footemen nexte about her highnes litter barehed

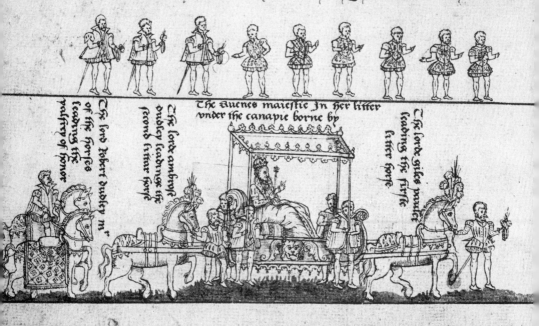

The Quenes maiestie in her litter vnder the canapie borne by

The lord Robert dudley mr of the horses leadinge the pallory of honor

The lord ambrose dudley leadinge the second litter horse

The lord giles paulet leadinge the firste litter horse

The Quieres and footemen nexte aboute her highnes litter barehed

The genf pencionars on foote withe pollapes in their handes barehed

The maior of london barefied

The duke of norffolcke mareshall of england barefied

Garter chyffe kinge off armes barefied

The sworde borne by therle of barefied

Therle of oxford lorde greate chamberlain of england barefied

The gent vsher of the prye chamber barefied

Sargeauntis at armes

denote that their wearers were kings *of arms*. A book of arms of Knights of the Garter made about 1430 by William Bruges, the first Garter King of Arms, shows him wearing such a crown (Plate VIII).

The ceremonies of the Order of the Garter must be among the first which we can feel sure that heralds conducted, but the first pictures of English heralds at ceremonial work, though produced by or for John Writhe, Garter 1478-1504, relate to the ceremonies of creation of Knights of the Bath, which were indeed of a complexity to require professional assistance (cf. Plate XII). The vast heraldic *oeuvre* of Writhe's son and successor Sir Thomas Wriothesley comprises pictorial as well as written record of some of the ceremonies he had a part in. His great Roll of the Westminster Tournament of 1511 arguably comes under this head. The Roll of the Procession to the Parliament of 1512 at Trinity College, Cambridge (Plate XI), decidedly does so, as do the drawings at the College of Arms of his father dining with the future Emperor Maximilian in 1490 and himself dining with the Emperor Ferdinand I at Nuremberg in 1523 after their respective investitures with the Garter (Plate X). Also there is the drawing at Windsor of Henry VIII's Opening of Parliament of 1523.

A series of ceremonial records or guides in the form of lively pen and ink sketches of processions and the like was produced mainly for Sir Gilbert Dethick, Garter 1550-84, and is now divided between the College of Arms (26) and the British Library, apart from a diagram of the 1553 parliament at Windsor. There have of course been certain historically important changes, but many arrangements shown in these formularies continue little if at all changed today (27).

27   Heralds at the Coronation of Queen Elizabeth II 2 June 1953. Behind and to the right of Sir Winston Churchill are H.S. London, Norfolk Herald Extraordinary and Dermot Morrah, Arundel Herald Extraordinary. Behind them are A. R. Wagner, Richmond Herald, now Garter, Sir Thomas Innes of Learney, Lyon King of Arms, and R. P. Graham-Vivian, Windsor Herald and later Norroy and Ulster King of Arms. Further back are A. G. B. Russell, Lancaster Herald, later Clarenceux King of Arms, and A. J. Toppin, York Herald, later Norroy and Ulster King of Arms.

The Introductions of new peers into the House of Lords, conducted by Garter, follow a form of such antiquity that its origin had been forgotten when in 1964 a crisis arose. The number of Life Peers then being created was so much greater than usual that the machinery showed signs of strain and it was suggested that some drastic change in the arrangements must be made. But before this could be done, it was necessary to know by whom and by what authority these arrangements had originally been made and research to this end was called for. This research brought to light that the present form is a much simplified and shortened digest of much older forms, which was laid down in 1621, when the King had just made Thomas, Earl of Arundel, Earl Marshal. The reason for the change was that it had become known that the King was granting peerages for substantial cash consideration and the criticism this attracted made the old form of investiture by the king himself embarrassing to him. To establish these facts took more than a year and in the meantime the 1964 crisis was over (*OIP*).

One investiture only, that of the Prince of Wales, is still conducted in the pre-1621 peerage form and like investitures of peers before 1621 does not necessarily take place in Parliament (28). On the last two occasions (1911 and 1969), the Sovereign has held it at Caernarvon Castle. The Earl Marshal as of old was in charge of the proceedings and the heralds helped him both to prepare and conduct them.

The first full pictorial treatment of the Coronation proceedings is the great book of the Coronation of James II which Francis Sandford, Lancaster Herald, produced in 1687, with much help, it is said, from Gregory King (29). Sir George Nayler, Garter, embarked upon, but did not live to finish, a still more ambitious colour plate record of the 1820 Coronation of George IV. For the preparation of

28 Diagrammatic drawing of the entry procession for the investiture of Henry Prince of Wales in the Court of Requests, 1610. College of Arms. MS. WA. f. 47. First in the procession approaching the King comes Sir William Segar, Garter, bearing the letters patent; then five peers with the robe, the sword, the ring, the rod and the coronet; last the prince between two dukes. *OTP* Pl. XXI, pp. 134, 140.

47

The Queenes
Mo: and her
Children

Ambassa

Trumpetts

Bishops, in number Nine.

*Portcullis Blewma
Pursuivant. Pursuiva*

29 Bishops followed by two pursuivants, Thomas Holford, Portcullis, and John Gibbon, Bluemantle (their tabards now no longer worn athwart; see p. 68), at the Coronation of King James II, 1685. From *The History of the Coronation of . . . James II,* by Francis Sandford, Lancaster Herald, 1687, with engravings by William Sherwin, Nicholas Yeates and John Collins (see p. 76). At the funeral of the Duke of Albemarle in 1670 the 'comely and cheerful appearance' of Mr Holford is said to have made King Charles II and many others laugh heartily (MS note by J. C. Brooke quoting John Gibbon).

coronations a special Earl Marshal's Office, framed on the heralds (27), is now set up about a year before the event.

Of the other ceremonies in which heralds have been employed by far the most frequent have been funerals, and this not only of sovereigns, royalty and the great, but in former times of the nobility and gentry at large. 'Goe to the Heralds Office', said John Donne preaching in St Paul's on Christmas Day 1627, 'Goe to the Heralds Office, the spheare and element of Honour, and thou shalt finde those men as busie there about the consideration of Funerals, as about the consideration of Creations: thou shalte finde that office to be as well the Grave as the Cradle of Honour: and thou shalt finde in that Office as many Records of attainted families and impoverished and forgotten, and obliterate families, as of families newly created and presently celebrated'.

How this had come about is a little puzzling but seems to be linked with a change to be seen in the later fourteenth and the fifteenth century, from heraldry on tombs, which merely identified the deceased, to a heraldic display on them of descents and alliances. It was natural that heralds should at that time be introduced into the funerals of those noblemen who retained heralds. Part of their function on these occasions was to carry the armour of the deceased, the coat of arms, sword, shield, crest, helmet and spurs, which were then hung over the tomb. The carrying and hanging up of armour at funerals itself no doubt goes back much further, but the first record I have seen of English heralds officiating at a funeral is at that of Richard Neville, Earl of Salisbury, and his son Sir Thomas at Bisham in 1463. The oldest surviving English examples of funeral armour, including shield, helm and crest, are those of Edward Prince of Wales (the Black Prince), of 1376. Until recently they hung above his tomb in Canterbury Cathedral and are now displayed near by while replicas take their original place. There are notable examples on the Continent, as at Marburg.

Down to 1500 the recorded heraldic funerals are of princes and great nobles, but in 1504 the heralds marshalled that of Sir John Shaa, Alderman of London. By the middle of the sixteenth century the custom had spread down to knights and citizens and their ladies and before its end to the richer gentry. The heralds attending on such occasions recorded funeral certificates, of which an extensive series is preserved in the College. The proceedings on such occasions were regulated by orders, revised from time to time by the Earl Marshal, laying down among other things the form and scale of mourning and heraldic display appropriate to different ranks (Plate XV).

Thomas Lant (*c.* 1556-1601) entered the personal service of Sir Philip Sydney about 1583. He went with him to the Low Countries and was there in 1586 when Sir Philip died of wounds received at the relief of Zutphen. Returning to England, Lant was employed by Secretary Walsingham, by whose recommendation and that of Lord Leicester to the Earl Marshal, he was appointed Portcullis Pursuivant in

1588, becoming Windsor Herald in 1597. Sydney had been accorded a great funeral procession to St Paul's where he was buried. Lant had published in 1587 an elaborate pictorial record of this engraved on thirty four plates by Theodore de Bry (30).

30   Heralds in the procession to the funeral of Sir Philip Sydney at St Paul's Cathedral 17 October 1586. From the roll prepared by his servant Thomas Lant, afterwards Portcullis Pursuivant (1588-97) and Windsor Herald (1597-1600). The fifth from the left is Robert Glover, Somerset. Engraved on thirty four plates by Theodore de Bry, printed 1587. A. M. Hind, *Engraving in England in the sixteenth and seventeenth centuries*. Pt. I. The Tudor Period, Pl. XVI, 132-7; *HCEC* No. 9. Pl. XV; *HE* Pl. XVIII.

31 Kings of arms and heralds bearing the achievements of the deceased in the funeral procession of George Monck, Duke of Albemarle, 1670. Plate 16 of the engraved procession collected by Francis Sandford, Rouge Dragon (afterwards Lancaster). F. Barlow invenét. Robert White sculpsit (p. 84). *HE* Pl. XXX.

Ashmole Esq.
Windsor
Herald.

William Dugdale Esq.
Norroy King
of Armes.

Sr. Edward Bysshe Kt.
Clarenceux
King of
Armes.

Sr. Edward Carteret
Kt. one of his Maties.
Gentlemen Ushers.

16

In 1670 George Monck, whose part in the Restoration of King Charles II in 1660 had been recognized by creating him Duke of Albemarle, was accorded a state funeral in Westminster Abbey (already mentioned on page 53) of grandeur comparable to Sydney's. This in its turn was recorded in a series of engraved plates edited by Francis Sandford, Rouge Dragon, and published under royal authority (31).

Twelve years earlier the heralds had conducted a comparably splendid funeral of which one would much like to have a pictorial record, that of the Lord Protector, Oliver Cromwell, in Westminster Abbey. We are told that its total cost was £28,000 (*DI* p. 285 quoting British Library Harl. MSS. 1372 p. 2 and 1438 pp. 8 and 10; *PR* pp. 181-203). There were six great banners wrought on rich taffaty in oil and gilt with fine gold and silver at £6 apiece; three large achievements in oil, two yards long, with mantle, helmet and crest, supporters and motto, gilt with fine gold at £15 apiece; his shield, painted in oil and richly gilt with a crown with fine gold; a crest, carved with a golden lion standing upon a regal crown; at the feet of the effigies: two lions, carved and gilded with fine gold, with crowns, and two dragons, wrought in oil; sixteen cast crowns, fixed on the uprights, gilt with fine gold; fifty taffaty escucheons, gilt with fine gold and silver, with crowns, for the horses and chariot, at 10s. a piece; and much more of the same sort. Thus the royal crown which Oliver refused in life was accorded him in death.

Heraldic funerals remained in fashion for the gentry till about the 1670s and for some of the nobility down to about 1690. Thereafter they grew very rare and were eventually confined to those of royalty, some very great noblemen and to state funerals at the public expense. Among the last named were those of the Earl of Chatham, 1778, Lord Nelson and William Pitt, 1806, the Duke of Wellington, 1852, Mr Gladstone, 1898, and Sir Winston Spencer Churchill, 1965. At this last, as on earlier occasions, the heraldic achievements were carried by the heralds in St Paul's Cathedral.

And now having followed a clue which has joined for us into one historical sequence the heralds' concern with tournaments, armorial bearings, ancestors, pedigrees and ceremonies sad and joyful from funerals to coronations, we will ask one more question. Are this link and sequence mere accidents of history or have they a deeper inherent logic? Do these activities, diverse as they are, all in their different ways belong to and express a certain aspect of life or attitude towards it?

'Man is a noble animal', wrote Dugdale's friend Sir Thomas Browne, 'splendid in ashes and pompous in the grave, solemnizing nativities and deaths with equal lustre, nor omitting ceremonies of bravery in the infamy of his nature'. But, he added, 'We drive not at ancient families . . . We honour your old virtues, conformable unto times before you, which are the noblest armoury'. So Thomas Gray's reflection on the boast of heraldry may be balanced by a not less heraldic and more rousing *envoy* from Wordsworth:

It is not to be thought of that the Flood
    Of British freedom, which, to the open sea
Of the world's praise, from dark antiquity,
    Has flowed, 'with pomp of waters, unwithstood',
Roused though it be full often to a mood
    Which spurns the check of salutary bands,
That this most famous Stream in bogs and sands
    Should perish; and to evil and to good
Be lost forever. In our halls is hung
    Armoury of the invincible Knights of old.
We must be free or die, who speak the tongue
    That Shakespeare spake; the faith and morals hold
Which Milton held – In everything we are sprung
    Of Earth's first blood, have titles manifold.

BIBLIOGRAPHY AND ABBREVIATIONS

*ASP*II   *Aspilogia. Being materials of Heraldry.* General Editor, Sir Anthony Wagner, Hatleian Society and Society of Antiquaries.
I (See below *CEMRA*).
II *Rolls of Arms. Henry III.* T. D. Tremlett and H. S. London. Additions to *CEMRA* by Sir A. Wagner. 1967.

BHA   Burlington Fine Arts Club. *Catalogue of a Collection of Objects of British Heraldic Art.* 1916.

CA   *The College of Arms, Queen Victoria Street, being the sixteenth and final monograph of the London Survey Committee,* by Walter H. Godfrey, assisted by Sir Anthony Wagner, with a complete list of the Officers of Arms by H. Stanford London. 1963.

CEMRA   Aspilogia I (above). A. R. Wagner. *A Catalogue of English Mediaeval Rolls of Arms.* 1950.

CP   *The Complete Peerage.* By G.E.C. (G. E. Cokayne, Clarenceux King of Arms). New Edition Revised and much enlarged by Vicary Gibbs, H. A. Doubleday, Duncan Warrand, Lord Howard de Walden, Geoffrey H. White and R. S. Lea. 14 volumes. 1910-59.

DCD   D. C. Douglas, *English Scholars.* 1939.

DI   James Dallaway, *Inquiries into the Origin and Progress of the Science of Heraldry in England.* 1793.

DLG   D. L. Galbreath, *Manuel de Blason,* ed. Leon Jequier. Lausanne, 1977.

EG   A. R. Wagner, *English Genealogy,* 1st ed. 1960, 2nd. 1972. Page references to 2nd ed.

EHS   *English Historical Scholarship in the Sixteenth and Seventeenth Centuries.* ed. Levi Fox. 1956.

HCEC   *Heralds' Commemorative Exhibition 1484-1934 held at the College of Arms. Enlarged & Illustrated Catalogue.* 1936.

HE   A. R. Wagner, *Heralds of England.* 1967.

HH   A. R. Wagner. *Heralds and Heraldry in the Middle Ages.* 1st ed. 1939, 2nd. 1956. Page references to 2nd ed.

HHB   A. R. Wagner. *Historic Heraldry of Britain.* 1939.

L.W   Lynn White Jr. *Medieval Technology and Social Change.* 1962.

ME   *Medieval England,* ed. A. L. Poole. Oxford, 1958. Ch. XI. A. R. Wagner, 'Heraldry'.

OIP   *Archaeologia,* 101, 1967, Sir A. Wagner and J. C. Sainty 'The Origin of the Introduction of Peers in the House of Lords'.

PP   A. R. Wagner. *Pedigree and Progress.* 1975.

PR   *Prestwich's Respublica.* 1787.

PW   J. Enoch Powell and Keith Wallis. *The House of Lords in the Middle Ages.* 1968.

RCCA   A. R. Wagner. *The Records and Collections of the College of Arms.* 1952.

RFO   J. H. Round. *Family Origins,* ed. William Page. 1930.
RYWR   English Surnames Series, ed. R. A. McKinley, I. G. Redmonds. *Yorkshire West Riding.* 1973.
WSE   William Smith Ellis. *The Antiquities of Heraldry.* 1869.

ACKNOWLEDGEMENTS

The publishers are grateful to the author and to the College of Arms for allowing photographs to be taken of the material in their care, and to the photographers and institutions listed below for their help and cooperation in providing illustrations.

Giraudon, Paris: I; H. Sigros Edition Spes, Lausanne: II; John Webb, London: III, IV, V, IX, X, XIII, XV, 16, 17, 18, 19, 20, 21, 22, 23, 26, 28; Bibliothèque nationale, Paris: VI; VZW Levende Musea, Bruges: VII; Department of Manuscripts, the British Library: VIII; the Master and Fellows, Trinity College, Cambridge: XI; Fitzwilliam Museum, Cambridge (courtesy of the National Trust): XII; Martin Davison, Swindon (by courtesy of the Revd. Canon J. M. Free, Lydiard Millicent): XIV; Victoria and Albert Museum, London: 24, 25; Sport & General Press Agency, London: 27.